Euripides: Orestes

BLOOMSBURY COMPANIONS
TO GREEK AND ROMAN TRAGEDY

Series editor: Thomas Harrison

Aeschylus: Agamemnon Barbara Goward
Aeschylus: Persians David Rosenbloom
Aeschylus: Seven Against Thebes Isabelle Torrance
Euripides: Bacchae Sophie Mills
Euripides: Heracles Emma Griffiths
Euripides: Hippolytus Sophie Mills
Euripides: Ion Laura Swift
Euripides: Iphigenia at Aulis Pantelis Michelakis
Euripides: Medea William Allan
Euripides: Orestes Matthew Wright
Euripides: Phoenician Women Thalia Papadopoulou
Euripides: Suppliant Women Ian C. Storey
Euripides: Trojan Women Barbara Goff
Seneca: Phaedra Roland Mayer
Seneca: Thyestes P.J. Davis
Sophocles: Ajax Jon Hesk
Sophocles: Electra Michael Lloyd
Sophocles: Philoctetes Hanna Roisman
Sophocles: Women of Trachis Brad Levett

BLOOMSBURY COMPANIONS
TO GREEK AND ROMAN TRAGEDY

Euripides: Orestes

Matthew Wright

BLOOMSBURY
LONDON • NEW DELHI • NEW YORK • SYDNEY

Bloomsbury Academic
An imprint of Bloomsbury Publishing Plc

50 Bedford Square
London
WC1B 3DP
UK

1385 Broadway
New York
NY 10018
USA

www.bloomsbury.com

First published in 2008 by Gerald Duckworth & Co. Ltd.

© Matthew Wright 2008

Matthew Wright has asserted his right under the Copyright, Designs and Patents Act, 1988, to be identified as Author of this work.

All rights reserved. No part of this publication may be reproduced or transmitted in any form or by any means, electronic or mechanical, including photocopying, recording, or any information storage or retrieval system, without prior permission in writing from the publishers.

No responsibility for loss caused to any individual or organization acting on or refraining from action as a result of the material in this publication can be accepted by Bloomsbury or the author.

British Library Cataloguing-in-Publication Data
A catalogue record for this book is available from the British Library.

ISBN: PB: 978-0-7156-3714-2
ePUB: 978-1-4725-2125-5
ePDF: 978-1-4725-2126-2

Library of Congress Cataloging-in-Publication Data
A catalog record for this book is available from the Library of Congress.

Typeset by Ray Davies

Contents

Preface	7
1. Setting the Scene	9
2. Dramatic Structure and Performance	29
3. Humans and Gods	51
4. Late Euripides	72
5. Politics	90
6. Euripides' Cleverest Play	115
Notes	139
Guide to Further Reading	153
Bibliography	159
Glossary	167
Chronology	171
Index	173

Preface

Orestes is (in my view, at least) a splendid play, and this Companion is intended to make it accessible to a wider audience. In particular, I have tried to write the sort of book that my own undergraduates at the University of Exeter might find useful, but it is aimed more broadly at students, actors, directors, general readers and any who are approaching tragedy for the first time.

All the Greek is translated or paraphrased. (There are so many translations on the market that I have thought it best to supply my own, literal versions, but the line numbers should make them easy enough to use alongside any other translation.) The meaning of any unfamiliar or technical terms, where not explicitly given in the text, will be found in the Glossary, and the Notes and the Guide to Further Reading are designed to give additional help.

It is a pleasure to acknowledge the encouragement and support which I have received from many people. I shall not mention them all by name, in case I should accidentally leave someone out, but particular gratitude is due to my parents and to my friends Tony and Gill Yates, who made sure that I was well-nourished and in tolerably good spirits during the final stages of writing.

This book is dedicated to the memory of Graham Robertson, who first introduced me to Euripides. He was a remarkable man and is much missed by those who knew him.

Topsham   M.E.W.
August 2008

1

Setting the Scene

Euripides' *Orestes* was first performed in the spring of 408 BC, in the open-air Theatre of Dionysus at Athens. Its performance took place as part of the Athenian festival called the Greater (or City) Dionysia. This festival, in honour of the god Dionysus, took place every year, in the month of Elaphebolion (roughly equivalent to March in our calendar). By the fifth century BC, and for many years afterwards, it was a major public event, lasting for a whole week, involving religious rituals, political ceremonies, processions, feasting and drinking, as well as various types of dramatic and musical performance.[1]

Orestes was not the only tragedy performed on this occasion. In fact, there would have been as many as seventeen plays produced during each festival. Between three and five comic playwrights would each have offered a comedy, while three tragic playwrights would each have presented a set of four plays, comprising three tragedies and one satyr-play (a bawdy sort of drama, named after its chorus of 'satyrs' or wild men). A prize was awarded to the playwright judged to be the best in each category.

It would be nice to think that Euripides won the prize in 408 – but, sadly, we do not know who won, or even who were the other competitors, tragic or comic. Nor do we know the titles of the other tragedies and satyr-play which Euripides wrote to accompany *Orestes*. It is also impossible to know whether this set of three or four plays were all part of a continuous narrative, or whether they were thematically connected in some other way (though *Orestes* does seem to be a free-standing, self-contained work).[2] Indeed – as anyone who spends any time at all studying

Euripides: Orestes

ancient Greece will soon realize – there is an awful lot that we simply do not know. The only reason we can be sure that *Orestes* dates from 408 is because a scholiast – that is, an anonymous ancient scholar whose marginal commentary on the text has been preserved in the manuscript tradition – happens to tell us, in his note on line 371, that Diocles was archon of Athens at the time of the first performance.

The author of *Orestes*

Reliable information about the life and career of Euripides is similarly hard to come by. Our evidence comes from a very miscellaneous and untrustworthy collection of ancient biographies, including the anonymous *Lineage and Life of Euripides*, Thomas Magister's mediaeval *Life of Euripides*, the fragments of Satyrus' *Life* (written in dialogue form), the entry in the *Souda* (a tenth-century encyclopaedia) and various snippets contained in ancient commentaries and other sources.[3] Most of these sources, which date from much later than the period they describe, are inaccurate, anecdotal, scabrous and gossipy, and they appear to have used a common range of source-material, since they mostly duplicate one another. It has been shown that nearly all of the 'factual' information in the biographies is actually derived from the caricature-portraits of Euripides in ancient comedy, or even from the plots of Euripides' plays themselves.[4] These sources, which describe Euripides' rise to fame from humble origins, his relationship with Socrates, his complicated sex-life, and his gory death – are certainly worth a read, but they must be treated as entertaining works of fiction.

Nevertheless, there are a few genuine facts that can be pieced together. Euripides was born around 485-480 BC in Athens, and died in 406 in Macedon (where he had gone as court poet to king Archelaus). The plot of Aristophanes' comedy *Frogs*, which was produced in 405, centres on Dionysus' descent to the Underworld in order to bring back Euripides from the dead. During his long life Euripides wrote more than ninety plays, of which eighteen survive – the best known being *Medea,*

1. Setting the Scene

Hippolytus, Heracles and *Bacchae*. (A nineteenth, *Rhesus*, handed down to us along with Euripides' work, is now usually thought to be the work of a different author.) Euripides first produced plays in 455 BC, but all of the works that survive date from his middle and later period. His earliest extant tragedy is *Alcestis* (438), while other securely datable plays apart from *Orestes* include *Medea* (431), *Trojan Women* (415), *Helen* (412), and the posthumous *Iphigenia at Aulis* and *Bacchae* (405-4). Most of the others have to be dated by a process of educated guesswork (based on the plays' content and style).[5]

Euripides won fewer prizes than some of his rivals: he was awarded first prize on five occasions (one of them posthumously in 404), which compares unfavourably with (for example) Sophocles' twenty-two victories. Nevertheless, Euripides evidently enjoyed great popularity and fame: to appreciate this, one only has to look at the number of times that he featured in contemporary comedies by Aristophanes and others, or the frequency with which his plays were quoted and discussed by writers throughout antiquity. From all of these sources it is clear that Euripides was perceived as a writer of sophisticated, innovative and often controversial drama.

We may not be able to say very much with confidence about Euripides' life, but it is clear, at least, that *Orestes* is a work of its author's old age; it is also one of the very latest Greek tragedies that survives to the present day. Both of these facts need to be kept firmly in mind: as we shall see later on, they are highly significant when it comes to understanding the play's critical reception. First, however, it is worth saying a few introductory words about the genre of drama to which *Orestes* belongs.

Athenian *tragôidia*

The words 'tragedy' and 'tragic', in modern usage, are complex and potent terms which are applied to a wide variety of different phenomena in literature and life. But for an Athenian of the fifth century, a tragedy – *tragôidia* in Greek – was simply a play based on mythical or historical subject-matter, staged at one of the city's religious festivals such as the Greater Dionysia or the Lenaea.

The subject-matter of *tragôidia* is as varied as the Greek myths themselves, but there is a preference for story-patterns involving intra-familial conflict and the perversion of ritual.[6] Within these broad limits there is much scope for different types of plot, and it is hard to discern any 'common denominator' to plays as varied as (say) *Seven Against Thebes, Prometheus Bound, Philoctetes, Medea, The Children of Heracles* and *Orestes*. It is easier to generalize about the sort of emotions experienced by the characters in *tragôidia* than it is to generalize about the sort of thing that happens to them: invariably the plays depict men and women caught in the grip of strong feelings such as fear, anger, love, hatred, madness, sorrow and anguish.

Some Greek tragedies end happily, others end unhappily; some are full of deaths, while in others no one dies; some seem to centre on a single 'heroic' character, others do not. So far as there is any common outlook or meaning at all to the tragedies, they are all concerned (to varying degrees) with the Greek gods whom the audience worshipped and to whom they performed ritual. Invariably the plays explore aspects of human suffering, in relation to what was known or believed about these gods. Despite the fact that drama was performed at festivals of Dionysus, scholars have never been able to agree whether or not there is anything intrinsically Dionysiac in its nature.[7] At any rate, the god of the theatre plays no obvious role in *Orestes* (and is conspicuous by his absence from most other tragedies – apart from the *Bacchae*, of course). Since the Greater Dionysia was, in a very prominent sense, a *political* as well as a religious occasion in the life of the city, scholars also continue to argue about whether or not there is any political significance to *tragôidia*. (I explore the politics of Greek tragedy in more detail, with specific reference to *Orestes*, in Chapter 5 below.)

Tragôidia in performance was minimalist, highly formal and stylized, with little attempt to create realism.[8] All the plays

1. Setting the Scene

were designed to be performed by a cast of two or three masked male actors, who played all the roles between them, and a chorus of singers and dancers. The plays were performed in an outdoor theatre, with minimal scenery and scarcely any props, in front of an audience of up to around fifteen thousand people. It is worth stressing, since it is not always clear from modern editions and translations, that *tragôidia* was musical theatre, composed entirely in verse: the plays are made up of a mixture of spoken dialogue, recitative, solo song and various types of choral odes accompanied by woodwind music, percussion and dancing. (I return to the issue of performance at greater length in the next chapter.)

We now possess so few surviving examples of *tragôidia* that it is dangerous to generalize too much. However, it is clear that the genre developed during the fifth century. *Orestes* is one of the very latest extant tragedies, and it seems that Euripides' audience in 408 could expect to be presented with something rather different from, say, Aeschylus' *Persians* (our earliest extant tragedy, over sixty years earlier). The most obvious developments took place in the area of performance. For instance, in the later tragedies the chorus is used far more fluidly, with a greater variety of types of song and dance, than in Aeschylus or earlier Sophocles. Euripides, in particular, developed a penchant for including actors' solo song (to such an extent that Aristophanes parodied his monodic style in the comedy *Frogs*), thus bringing tragedy closer to what we would think of as an 'operatic' form. On the level of plot, later plays tend to involve far more action (as opposed to talking), increased use of the stage-building (*skênê*) and stage-machinery, and a greater number of surprises, twists and turns. One consequence of this increased amount of action seems to be that plays on average became longer and longer (*Orestes*, at a bumper 1693 lines, is one of the longest as well as one of the latest extant tragedies).

All of these 'late' features are visible in *Orestes*, which features a complex structure with several recognitions and reversals, a murder plot, a roof-top hostage scenario, at least

Euripides: Orestes

one surprise entry using the mechanical crane (*mêchanê*), spectacular tableau-scenes at the beginning and end of the play, a personal appearance by the god Apollo, a large amount of varied singing and dancing, and an extensive role for the solo performer who delivers the 'messenger speech' in the form of an elaborate operatic aria.

There are other ways in which *Orestes* may be seen as a 'late' work of its author, but I shall come back to this subject in Chapter 4 below. What is important for now is that although, on the face of it, *Orestes* may strike us as being very different in some ways from other well-known tragedies such as *Medea*, *Agamemnon* or *Oedipus the King* (or, for that matter, *King Lear*), it does fit the definition of *tragôidia* given above, and it can be situated clearly within the fifth-century development of the genre. My brief definition of *tragôidia* will probably seem rather lean to anyone who is used to contemplating 'the tragic' in a wider sense, but it is crucial to discard anachronistic notions of tragedy when studying purely Greek tragedy. The importance of this approach will become clear when we come to consider the play's reputation in modern times.

Orestes and its ancient and modern reception

This Companion, like the other volumes in the series, is designed to provide the reader with an introduction to the play and to the world of Greek tragedy in general. One of the other aims of the series is to describe the plays' 'reception' – their afterlife, in the form of subsequent performances, adaptations and quotations by later writers. But in this respect *Orestes* poses a special problem: for many years the play has been more or less ignored by writers, creative artists, theatre audiences, readers and the general public. In fact, the *lack* of modern popular reception is one of the most significant things about this play.

One of the most useful resources to have been created for scholars in recent years is the on-line Oxford Archive for the Performance of Greek and Roman Drama, which provides an

1. Setting the Scene

annotated list of all known performances of ancient drama.[9] A glance at the Archive's listings for *Orestes* shows that this play has been one of the least performed of all Greek tragedies. There has been a resurgence of interest during the last thirty years or so (as there has been in the case of Greek tragedy in general), and the play has lately been restaged, heavily adapted, cut or altered, a number of times in Europe, America and further afield; but during the previous two millennia it was almost never performed. (Astonishingly, the first ever professional production of *Orestes* in the UK did not take place until the late 1990s.[10]) Furthermore, *Orestes* does not seem to have inspired any other writer after antiquity. Of course, the *myth* of Orestes and his family has been the subject of numerous literary and dramatic works in modern times, but in all cases the Greek models invariably seem to be Aeschylus, Sophocles or Euripides' earlier tragedy *Iphigenia among the Taurians*.[11]

The visual arts tell a similar story. Even though classical myth in general, and the Atreid myth in particular, provided inspiration for many modern European artists from the Renaissance onwards, I have not been able to trace a single post-classical painting or sculpture which is based specifically upon the tragedy *Orestes*. Again, it is the *Oresteia* and *Iphigenia among the Taurians*, as far as we can tell, that the artists seem to have had in mind.

Orestes is not a play that most people nowadays would immediately name if they were asked to think of a Greek tragedy. It is not thought of as a 'canonical' tragedy, such as *Antigone*, *Oedipus the King* or *Medea*. Indeed, many people, even classicists, have never read it, and it tends to be absent from school and university syllabuses.

In antiquity, by contrast, *Orestes* was one of its author's most admired and well-known tragedies. In the decades immediately following its first production, it was frequently talked about, quoted and parodied – a sure sign of its popular acclaim and importance.[12] The comic poet Strattis even devoted an entire play to parodying it – the (now lost) *Anthroporestes*, in which a character described *Orestes* as Euripides' cleverest and most

Euripides: Orestes

sophisticated drama.[13] The fourth-century comic playwright Menander also included echoes and parodies of the Argive assembly scene in his play *The Man from Sicyon*, which shows that Euripides' play was still well known to audiences some decades later.

Indeed, the evidence of epigraphy and ancient scholarship shows that *Orestes* was repeatedly re-performed, in Athens and elsewhere in the Greek world, from the fourth century BC onwards.[14] We have inscriptions which record at least two performances of *Orestes*: one at the Dionysia of 340, in which the main role was taken by the famous 'star' actor Neoptolemus, and another at the Dionysia of *c*. 276-219 BC – by this date the festival included revivals of 'classic' plays as well as new works. But there will doubtless have been very many more versions, in Athens and further afield. Ancient commentators on the play repeatedly refer to the staging of scenes in various productions, and, in particular, to alterations made to the text by later actors and producers (a topic to which we shall return in the next chapter when considering the play's staging).[15]

Orestes was also well known among readers and devotees of the theatre in Roman times. For instance, Vergil's memorable description of Queen Dido's distraught and frantic state of mind after being abandoned by Aeneas (*Aeneid* 4. 469-73) is based on vivid imagery taken from two Euripidean plays:

> She was in the state of Pentheus when, with mind deranged, he saw the Furies advancing in ranks, two suns appearing in the sky, and two cities of Thebes; or of Agamemnon's tormented son Orestes on the theatre-stage, seeking to escape a mother armed with firebrands and black snakes, while the avenging Spirits of the Curse wait at the door.[16]

The reference to 'the theatre-stage' makes it clear that this is not just an allusion to myth in general; rather, it depends on Vergil's readers being thoroughly familiar with Euripides' *Orestes* and *Bacchae* in particular. And the play's popularity was

1. Setting the Scene

not restricted to the Augustan city of Rome, but extended further across the Roman world. Another piece of evidence of a rather different sort – a wall-painting from a Roman house at Ephesus depicting the play's opening scene – shows that *Orestes* was familiar to inhabitants of Asia Minor in the second century AD.[17]

Aside from its history as a theatrical work in performance, *Orestes* remained popular throughout classical and later antiquity as a literary text for study by scholars and students.[18] It was chosen by Alexandrian scholars as one of the ten plays in their 'selected edition' of Euripides' works, and it was (along with *Hecuba* and *Phoenician Women*) one of the so-called 'Byzantine triad' of plays, chosen for their perceived educational value. This may partly explain why we are fortunate enough to possess the complete text of *Orestes* in a reasonably good state, while so many other works of Greek drama and literature have been lost: it was very extensively copied and circulated over a wide extent of time and space. There are nearly *ten times* more manuscripts of the 'Byzantine triad' than of the other plays of Euripides – a highly significant statistic. There also exist, in the works of other Latin and Greek authors, more quotations and citations of *Orestes* than of any other Greek drama – an extraordinary fact which illustrates, again, the high status which the play once enjoyed among men of letters.

How are we to account for the fact that *Orestes* became so unpopular in modern times? It cannot be due to its subject-matter: after all, the House of Atreus is the basis for other, more widely appreciated, ancient tragedies (including Aeschylus' *Oresteia* and the *Electra* plays by both Sophocles and Euripides), and it has inspired great modern works of art (such as Richard Strauss's *Elektra*, Darius Milhaud's *Agamemnon* and Eugene O'Neill's *Mourning Becomes Electra*, to name but a few). It is not that the myth itself has lost its appeal. And the play itself (as I hope to show in the chapters that follow) offers a good deal of interest and variety. Its plot, which centres on the grim aftermath of Orestes' murder of his mother Clytemnestra, is exciting and well structured, as well as morally complex; its

Euripides: Orestes

presentation of disease and insanity is unusually intense and disturbing; it deals with politics in a way which seems to have deep resonances for both ancient and modern democracies; its theatrical and musical effects are remarkable; and it has a brilliantly unexpected and ironic ending.

In spite of all this, the play has not been widely admired. While artists and the general public have on the whole neglected *Orestes*, the world of scholarship, on the other hand, has tended to undervalue or disparage it. 'Not many people, if asked to nominate the greatest Greek tragedy, would choose *Orestes*.' So writes Martin West, the author of the most recent critical edition of this play. He is reflecting the views of many generations of readers and critics. Indeed, anyone who reads any of the scholarly literature on *Orestes* will be struck immediately by the predominance of negative views of one sort or another. The play has been thought 'baffling', 'puzzling', 'inferior', 'vulgar', 'mediocre', 'not one of the most commendable, but rather one of the most difficult tragedies of this difficult dramatist', 'a melodrama, imagined sensationally, not tragically'; '*Orestes* produces for so many a sense not of pity but of profound revulsion', 'it is not a play that anyone can enjoy', and so on.[19] In this book I want to show that, on the contrary, *Orestes* is a play that *can* be enjoyed – and admired. But one cannot do that without also exploring some of the reasons underlying the play's poor reputation.

Genre and other problems

It may well be that there is a connection between the play's lack of *popular* reception and its predominantly negative *critical* reception from scholars. But I believe that the play's troubled reception is not really due to any perceived lack of interest or faults in design. When we read further in the secondary literature, we emerge with an overwhelming sense that the critics have disliked *Orestes* not because it is simply 'bad' (whatever that might mean), but because they do not think it succeeds properly *as a tragedy*. There have been a number of variations

1. Setting the Scene

on this position.[20] Sometimes Euripides has been disparaged for trying and failing to write a proper tragedy (the view of most nineteenth- and twentieth-century scholars), or he has been criticized for having deliberately set out to *destroy* tragedy (the view famously expressed by Nietzsche in *The Birth of Tragedy*).[21] More recently, many have suggested that Euripides in *Orestes* (and other late works, including *Helen* and *Ion*) was deliberately experimenting with genre, transforming tragedy into some new or hybrid type of drama. If this is true, we may choose to condemn him (for undermining the dignity and purity of the form) or actually admire him (for demonstrating a very modern-seeming, genre-bending literary sophistication).[22] Either way, one often finds *Orestes* and these other plays being described as 'tragicomedies', 'melodramas' or 'romances' – genres which in fact were only invented at different periods later in the history of literature.[23]

It is clear that *Orestes* does not conform to modern audiences' expectations of what a 'tragedy' should be. Many people today – including scholars, students, theatregoers and members of the general public – have a quite definite idea of what is meant by 'tragedy'. However, our ideas tend to be based not purely on Greek *tragôidia* but on all sorts of other sources as well, including (for instance) Seneca, Shakespeare, Racine, Corneille, Dryden, Wagner – or just a general, rather hazy sense of 'the Tragic' as a characteristic of the human condition in general. Or perhaps our tastes have been formed on the basis of Aristotle's well-known preference for tragedies like *Oedipus the King*, or the (not entirely Aristotelian) ideas of fatal flaws, tragic errors, heroes, catastrophic downfalls, and so on.[24]

Whatever the reason, we usually expect our 'tragedies' to be full of death, incest, murder, suicide, ruin, fear and gloom, and we anticipate that events will normally end disastrously for the main characters. This is why we tend to prefer plays such as *Medea* and *Bacchae*. Naturally, then, we will be disconcerted by a tragedy such as *Orestes*. Here no one commits suicide, no one is murdered (apparently),[25] and no one suffers a downfall. At times it seems possible that such terrible events will occur, but

Euripides: Orestes

as it turns out there is an apparently happy ending: the plot culminates in marriage and reconciliation, rather than disaster and death. Nor is there, as we might expect from earlier dramatizations of Orestes' story, a prevailing atmosphere of misery and terror. Indeed, in several places (above all, the prologue, the scene featuring the Phrygian slave, and the rooftop *dénouement*) it even comes close to being quite funny, and many other passages are marked by a peculiarly self-conscious, ironical, even playful tone.[26]

However, the crucial factor in all of this is that 'tragedy' (in the broader sense) and Greek *tragôidia* (in the more limited sense that I described above) are different sorts of entity. Significantly, Euripides' other so-called 'happy ending' tragedies, such as *Ion* and *Iphigenia among the Taurians*, have also been thought to be 'untragic', and have also suffered a comparative lack of modern popular reception, though like *Orestes* they were hugely popular in antiquity.

Anyone coming afresh to *Orestes* – or anything that has been written on it – needs to be aware at the outset of the problem of genre. In a sense, of course, it is a *non*-problem, in that it would never have occurred to Euripides or his audience to question for a moment the fact that his play was a *tragôidia*. Nevertheless, it is the most commonly encountered theme in the secondary literature on the play. Most scholars have, in different ways, made genre central to their interpretation – as if the question 'is this tragic or not?' was always at the front of Euripides' (or his audience's) thoughts. But fifth-century Athenians were far less preoccupied with genre than we are.

That is not to say that the question of genre is the only one that has occupied the play's critics. Another job that this book will try to do, as it moves through the thematic chapters which follow, is to introduce readers to some of the other main strands in the modern critical literature. It will be obvious that scholars have tended to find fault with *Orestes* on a number of grounds. Its plot-structure (discussed in Chapter 2) has come in for particular criticism, with many readers seeing it as chaotic or badly put together. The play's human characters have been

1. Setting the Scene

criticized for their supposed moral turpitude, while their attitude towards the gods has been called unorthodox (Chapter 3). The play's overall conception has been condemned as decadent by many scholars, following Friedrich Nietzsche's famous discussion of 'late Euripides' in *The Birth of Tragedy*: in Chapter 4 I argue that the issue of the play's 'lateness', like that of its genre, is of central importance for understanding the play and its reception. Chapter 5 deals with the play's political aspects and different ways of interpreting tragic politics. Finally Chapter 6 discusses *Orestes* in relation to its intellectual context – another issue which has tended to divide scholars, with some seeing Euripides as a profound thinker and others dismissing him as a superficial wit or intellectual joker.

What sort of play was Euripides trying to write, and how does it achieve its effects? Many of the problems that critics have had with the play can, to a large extent, be solved if we try to answer these questions with reference to Greek *tragoidia*, rather than some other conception of 'tragedy'. Throughout this book, I will be trying to imagine the play's impact on its original audience in 408 BC. What did they expect from a tragedy, and what would they have made of *Orestes*? Until further advances are made in the field of time-travel, we cannot give a definitive response to this question. Nevertheless, it seems to me that *Orestes* would have come across as a continually inventive, original and often odd play – but still a tragedy. Within the normal limits of his genre, Euripides seems to have been at pains to give his audience a new and challenging experience, even though this was a myth that they would have encountered many times before in drama and other forms of literature.

A new twist on old material

The story of Orestes and his terrible family was frequently told by poets and dramatists in archaic and classical Greece. It is not hard to understand why this should have been so, for the goings-on in the House of Atreus are grotesquely fascinating. Members of this doomed royal family included Orestes' great-

Euripides: Orestes

great-grandfather Tantalus, who stole ambrosia and nectar from Zeus himself, and was later reputed to have cut up and eaten his son Pelops; he was punished, according to most versions of the myth, by having a giant rock dangerously suspended above his head (though in *Orestes* Euripides tells a rather different story).[27] Pelops himself, having survived to inherit his father's throne, ran into trouble when he tried to marry Hippodameia, the daughter of Oenomaus, king of Pisa. Oenomaus forced Pelops to compete for Hippodameia's hand in a chariot-race; Pelops won the race, having bribed the king's charioteer Myrtilus to help him, but he later quarrelled with Myrtilus and killed him – and the dying Myrtilus put a curse on Pelops and his descendants.

Pelops' two sons, Thyestes and Atreus, were famous for their feud which culminated in Atreus' slaughtering several of Thyestes' children and serving them up to him for dinner. Atreus' son was Agamemnon, leader of the Greek expedition against Troy, husband of Clytemnestra, and father of Orestes, Electra and Iphigenia. In order for the Greeks to be able to set sail for war, Agamemnon was compelled by the goddess Artemis to sacrifice his daughter Iphigenia: he did this reluctantly, but in doing so incurred the wrath of Clytemnestra, who murdered him when he returned from the war. Clytemnestra was aided in the murder by her lover Aegisthus (one of Thyestes' sons who had managed to avoid being eaten). In order to avenge the spirit of Agamemnon, and spurred on by the instructions of the god Apollo, Orestes responded by killing his mother and Aegisthus.

It is clear even from this compressed summary that Orestes' family troubles are complicated and go back in time much further than the events described in our play. Both before and after Euripides' *Orestes* there were many re-tellings of the various stages in the story, which differed in numerous large and small details as each successive writer reinterpreted the myth and added his own perspective. A glance at any modern attempt to tell the whole story, such as Robert Graves' *Greek Myths* or an entry in *The Oxford Classical Dicionary*, shows how difficult or even impossible it is to reconstruct a single, 'author-

1. Setting the Scene

ized' version of the myth. In fact, Euripides himself often seems to be deliberately exploiting the fact that the mythical tradition was full of inconsistencies and alternatives, and suggesting that no one could ever really have accurate knowledge of all (or *any*) of the details.

Notable treatments of the myth before 408 included Homer's *Iliad* and *Odyssey*, which both contain numerous references to the family, even though they are not primarily concerned to narrate the whole story. Other, now lost, epic poems such as the *Cypria* and the *Nostoi* (or 'The Heroes' Returns') may have dealt with the myth in more depth.[28] The *Catalogue of Women*, a long genealogical poem attributed to Hesiod, narrates part of the story and, like Homer, was probably regarded as a particularly authoritative version. A particularly famous treatment of the story in antiquity was the *Oresteia* by the sixth-century Sicilian lyric poet Stesichorus: this work too is now, unfortunately, lost, but we know that (in common with the poet Pindar's eleventh *Pythian Ode*, which does survive) Stesichorus' poem dealt with Clytemnestra's motivation and her state of mind before and after murdering Agamemnon.

In the fifth century, Orestes and his family were among the most popular subjects for tragedy. Aeschylus' *Oresteia* (our only surviving tragic trilogy, consisting of *Agamemnon, Libation-Bearers* and *Eumenides*), produced for the first time in 458, seems to have become an almost instantaneous 'classic', and is an obvious model for later writers, including Euripides. Sophocles' tragedy *Electra* survives, but he also wrote other plays on the same theme, including *Atreus* and *Thyestes at Sicyon*; Euripides himself composed plays called *Electra, Oenomaus, Iphigenia at Aulis* and *Iphigenia among the Taurians*.

At numerous points in *Orestes* Euripides shows awareness of earlier versions, and (as we shall see in Chapter 4) he even seems to have designed this play as a 'sequel', of a sort, to his own and the other tragedians' previous works. Nevertheless, the really interesting thing about *Orestes* is that *none* of the events that take place on stage – Electra's treatment of the sick Orestes, the quarrel with Tyndareus, the civil disturbance at

Euripides: Orestes

Argos, the appearance of Helen and Menelaus with their daughter Hermione, and the murder-and-kidnap plan – is found in any previous version of the story. The play's action is (in the end) compatible with the myth in its usual form, but it consists of a stage in the story which is not dealt with by anyone else. It could be, of course, that Euripides based the plot on other lost material which we do not know about, but it seems more probable that he invented it. This is quite unusual, but not unparalleled: a number of other Euripidean plays, including *Ion, Iphigenia among the Taurians* and *Helen*, contain some material which is thought to be newly invented, while his younger contemporary, the tragedian Agathon, wrote a play (*Antheus* or *Anthos*) in which not only the plot but all the characters too were his own creations.

It is easy to imagine why Euripides should have felt the need to do something innovative with such familiar material. All tragedians, whose job it was to dramatize the traditional myths time and time again, must have felt increasing pressure to entertain and surprise their audiences. And yet *Orestes* seems to go somewhat further than most tragedies in this respect. In many ways it creates a distinctly odd, incongruous effect.

It is not only that the plot is made up. Other provocative touches include the surprising staging of certain scenes, the jarringly modern style of the music, and – most bizarrely of all – the fact that the play's action seems to be taking place in a version of modern-day Athens rather than ancient Argos. There is also something about the play's *tone* (a quality that is rather hard to define) that defies our expectations. We normally expect tragedy to be serious, intense and emotionally engaging, but at many points *Orestes* seems to be deliberately cultivating a tone of detachment and irony. We also expect drama to convince us, on its own terms, that the events presented on stage are real, but in *Orestes* the audience is repeatedly, self-consciously reminded that the play's 'reality' is actually *un*real, unbelievable – even, perhaps, absurd.

1. Setting the Scene

The prologue-speech as a scene-setting device

This incongruous, distancing tone is present from the very beginning of the play, in the prologue-speech delivered by Electra (1-70). Opening scenes in tragedy are nearly always of interest for their 'programmatic' qualities: they set the mood for the whole work and serve to orientate the audience, giving them a sense of the important themes and motifs. Many tragedies begin with a prologue-speech, a monologue delivered by one of the characters before anyone else enters the stage. Such monologues, among other functions, narrate the family background of the characters and give a plain, factual explanation of relevant events up to the point where the play's action begins.[29] Euripides was particularly fond of the device (seen also in *Medea, Alcestis, Helen, Hippolytus* and many other plays), though it was used by the other tragedians as well (e.g. Aeschylus' *Agamemnon*, Sophocles' *Women of Trachis* and so on).

The prologue-speech is always a difficult part of tragedy to evaluate. Although it is normally regarded as a soliloquy (itself a rather unrealistic convention of drama), it often seems as if the character is speaking directly to the audience. Many scholars are uncomfortable with this idea, because it is generally accepted that while comedy 'breaks the illusion', tragedy does not.[30] Still, it is hard to deny that prologue-speakers go some considerable way towards becoming detached narrator-figures: they display what looks very like a dispassionate, 'authorial' tone and a degree of knowledge (even seeming omniscience) which leaves them once the prologue has come to an end. When these characters are setting the scene, it can seem to us that they are not fully 'in character'.

Is this how it would have seemed to Euripides' audience? We cannot be quite sure. The question of what constitutes (or breaks) 'the illusion' in the non-naturalistic Greek theatre is far from straightforward,[31] and it is clear that audiences were well accustomed to the convention of the prologue-speech (however they might have interpreted these speeches). And yet in the prologue of *Orestes* in particular the overall effect of detachment

Euripides: Orestes

and unreality does seem to be more marked than in other prologues.

It is hard to resist the impression that Electra is primarily addressing the audience as such. This impression is reinforced by a couple of lines in particular: at 26, Electra refers to 'the public', and at the very end of the prologue, after Helen's exit, Electra asks: 'Did *you* see that ...?' (128), using a plural form of the verb which, since the chorus have not yet entered the stage, can only be addressed to the spectators. At the very point when we need to take in the details of the plot, Euripides deliberately undermines the reality of what is unfolding before us, reminding us that we are spectators sitting in a theatre and listening to an actor. Thus we can never *altogether* believe in the play's world – which inevitably affects our intellectual and emotional response to what happens.

The very first lines of the play, uttered by Electra as her brother Orestes lies, sick and unconscious, on a bed beside her, are:

> There is nothing that is so dreadful, to tell the tale or to suffer, nor is there any situation sent by a god, of which human nature is not liable to bear the burden (1-3).

Proverbial maxims (*gnômai*) of this sort are common in tragedy, but it is rare for a play to start with one. This particular *gnômê* is unusually cryptic in its sentiment and syntax: put more briefly, it seems to say that the gods are liable to cause humans any amount of suffering. To illustrate the point, Electra mentions her ancestor Tantalus, who (as I mentioned above) would have been well known to the audience for having a rock perpetually suspended above his head. However, the story as she tells it here (4-10) is different: Tantalus *himself*, she says, is suspended in mid-air along with the rock! Why has this small detail been altered? It distracts our attention from what seems to be the main subject (Tantalus' suffering).

As the commentators point out, the alteration probably constitutes an allusion to fifth-century scientific theories of

1. Setting the Scene

cosmology,[32] in which case Electra must be seen as 'updating' the myth in a weirdly anachronistic way. This sense of weirdness is enhanced not just by the details of the story (which Euripides, again, seems to have made up) but by the manner in which Electra tells it:

> The well-born Tantalus – no, I do not criticize him for his good fortune – son of Zeus – *so they say* – is now suspended in mid-air, dreading a rock which overhangs his head; he is being punished in this way – *so they say*, at least – because, a mortal among gods, having equal honour at their shared table, he caught a most shameful disease – an unguarded tongue (4-10).

What strikes us immediately is the hesitant, parenthetic style and the repeated phrase 'so they say', which undermines the credibility of the story.

'Distancing' techniques of this sort are seen elsewhere in the prologue-speech. In the middle of Electra's description of the family history, which includes the grisly story of her grandfather Atreus' butchering his brother's children, she breaks off (14) to pose a rhetorical question: 'Why do I need to rehearse all these obscenities?' The implication here, of course, is that the audience (to whom the question is implicitly addressed) knows the myth perfectly well already. The same apparent reluctance to speak of awful deeds is seen a couple of lines later, when Electra announces that she 'will pass over intervening events' (16). Again, these 'intervening events' are vital for understanding the play, but the spectators, who are familiar with the myths and have no doubt seen numerous tragedies on the same subjects, do not *need* to be told about them.

Electra continues with an account of her father Agamemnon's murder, and once again she makes reference to the fact that the story is already 'famous', almost as if she *knows* that they are all characters in a myth and not real-life people. Agamemnon is called 'the famous man – if indeed he *is* famous' (17), and his marriage to Clytemnestra is 'well-known through-

Euripides: Orestes

out Greece' (21). A little later, she describes her brother Orestes' murder of Clytemnestra as 'an act not glorious in the eyes of everybody' (30). This line draws our attention to the fact that the rights or wrongs of Orestes' behaviour had long been a subject for debate in literature and drama.

Similarly, when Electra is describing Clytemnestra's killing of Agamemnon, she again breaks off, saying: 'As for why she killed him, it is not proper for a young woman such as myself to say: *I leave that up to the public to decide*' (26-7). As before, her professed concern for decorum barely conceals the additional meaning of these bizarre lines. Clytemnestra's motivation for murdering her husband was in fact famously obscure – it had been presented very differently by the other tragedians, as well as lyric poets such as Stesichorus and Pindar – and Electra is archly acknowledging this. Her words here also highlight another surprising feature of *Orestes*: that is, a seeming indifference to the events which are supposed to constitute the moral centre of the play. (Everything turns on the consequences of the matricide, and Orestes' whole life is at stake: does it not *matter* how we evaluate Clytemnestra's actions?)

Whatever adjectives we use to describe Electra's tone – weird, self-conscious, sceptical, alienating, indifferent, ironic – it is clear that her prologue-speech is calculated to establish an unsettling and artificial mood for the play as a whole. This does not strike us as the tone normally adopted by someone who is personally involved in the awful experiences which she describes or alludes to. Even though Electra displays powerful emotions in the scenes which follow, here it can seem as if she does not believe, or even care about, what is happening. And so the audience, too, may well have found it difficult to believe entirely in what they saw and heard. Past events at Argos have been made to seem oddly unconvincing, and thus none of the subsequent action on stage ever comes across as *quite* real. As each successive scene in Euripides' newly invented plot unfolds, the overall sense of incongruity and strangeness increases.

2

Dramatic Structure and Performance

This chapter provides a scene-by-scene analysis of the play, concentrating particularly on the structure of the plot and the practicalities of performance. Since Euripides, like other tragedians, directed his own plays, it is appropriate to consider these two aspects side by side.

Of course, the play *could* be staged in any number of ways, given the flexibility and technical possibilities of the modern theatre. (Indeed, *Orestes* can often seem one of the most 'cinematic' tragedies: I have often thought it would work well in a film adaptation, directed by, say, Michelangelo Antonioni or David Lynch.) What I aim to do here is, in the first place, to consider how the play might have been put on at its original performance in the Theatre of Dionysus – but also, throughout the chapter, I compare and contrast various aspects of later productions of the play. As I pointed out in Chapter 1, *Orestes* has been staged much less often than other Greek tragedies, but a certain amount is known about performances of the play in the years since 408 BC. Looking at ways in which later directors have re-imagined the Euripidean original can throw new light on the play; it may also suggest further ideas for future productions.

The fifth-century Athenian stage

Much is uncertain: since no stage-directions survive in the manuscripts, our only evidence for staging comes from indications in the words of the play itself, together with our knowledge of the ancient theatre building and its paraphernalia.[1]

Euripides: Orestes

As I remarked in the previous chapter, fifth-century tragedy was minimalist in character. The performances took place outdoors, in the Theatre of Dionysus, which in the fifth century may have been rectangular or trapezoidal in shape (the semicircular theatre which survives on the site today is a later rebuilding).[2] From their tiered seats the spectators looked down upon a central stage (*orchêstra*) where the dancing and much of the action took place. At the rear of the *orchêstra* was the *skênê*, a building which could be used to represent a house, palace, temple, cave or whatever the play's setting might demand. The *skênê* had at least one set of double doors opening onto the *orchêstra*, and a flat roof which could be accessed by the actors. There was no 'curtain', and entrances and exits might be made from inside the *skênê* or from either of two passageways (*parodoi* or *eisodoi*) which led onto the *orchêstra* from stage right and stage left.

By the late fifth century, all the speaking roles in each tragedy were played by three male actors, who would change masks when moving between characters, accompanied by a chorus of twelve or fifteen singers and dancers. It seems that there was little attempt to create a visually realistic *mise-en-scène* with scenery or props, but inside (or concealed by) the *skênê* were two pieces of stage machinery which could be employed to create special effects. One of these, the *ekkyklêma*, was a miniature stage on wheels, which could be rolled out through the doors to represent an interior scene or tableau. The other, the *mêchanê*, is more difficult to picture in operation: it was clearly a sort of crane or harness, which seems to have been used for raising or lowering actors, creating the illusion of flight, or propelling characters suddenly into the audience's view (usually a *deus ex machina*, from which the Latin expression – 'the god from the crane' – is in fact derived).[3] We know, thanks to comic parodies,[4] that these devices were favoured by Euripides, but we cannot be quite certain how extensively or in which particular scenes they were used.

By today's standards, the style of classical Athenian theatre may seem alien, stilted and remarkably unspectacular. Never-

2. Dramatic Structure and Performance

theless, within its limits there was scope for creating striking theatrical effects. Since the playwrights were so restricted by formal convention, even slight innovations and departures from the norm could seem daring or dazzling.

Plot-structure

The structure of *Orestes* merits a few introductory remarks here because it has been one of the recurrent themes in the history of the play's critical reception. Many scholars have found fault with the design of the plot, which supposedly violates the Aristotelian principles of unity, probability and necessity, and which has been seen as episodic, chaotic or unconvincing.[5] But such criticism must be understood in its context. At one time it was conventional to disparage virtually *all* tragic plots except the classically 'perfect' *Oedipus the King* (which Aristotle in the *Poetics* held up as the example of a model plot), *Antigone, Agamemnon* and a few others. These plays do, it is true, exhibit a satisfyingly linear structure in which each successive scene leads on, relentlessly, to a seemingly inevitable conclusion. But there are very few situations, in myth or life, which could be turned into a plot-structure of this type, and it seems unnecessary for our view of what constitutes an acceptable or admirable plot to be restricted in this very narrow way.

Once again (as when thinking about tragedy or 'the tragic'), we ought not to base our expectations of the genre as a whole on *Oedipus* and a few other 'canonical' tragedies. It is worth stressing the fact that Aristotle's *Poetics*, however important it may have been in shaping later critical thinking about tragic plots, is a notoriously idiosyncratic document which does not represent 'mainstream' contemporary views.[6] Aristotle was writing in the fourth century BC, several decades later than the plays that he describes; and his views on tragedy, coloured by his own very particular and complex philosophical preoccupations, will have been very different from the views of Euripides or his audience.

What is a 'perfect' or 'unitary' plot in any case? The question

Euripides: Orestes

is very difficult, or even impossible, to answer. In the meantime, we may as well try to understand why Euripides structured his plot in the way that he did – unless we actually believe that 'Euripides set out to dramatize a situation, and it got the better of him'.[7] What is important is that a definite design *can* be perceived in the plot of *Orestes*: it is not simply a random, cobbled-together series of events. As we shall see from the analysis below, there is undeniably a change of direction in the middle of the play, but that does not mean that the principles of 'probable and necessary connection between events' have gone out of the window.

In fact, the play can be seen as a perfectly effective and fairly simple structure, falling into two halves. In the first half, Orestes and Electra are victims whose fate is to be decided, and it seems possible that Orestes will be driven out of his mind; they do not yet know what will be the decision of the Argive assembly regarding their future, and they hope for assistance from Menelaus or some other source. Later on, they learn both that the assembly has condemned them to death and that no help will be forthcoming, so that in the second half they are compelled to become active 'plotters' rather than passive victims. The *dénouement* results directly from the consequences of their (admittedly far-fetched and grotesque) scheme.

John Porter has drawn attention to the frequency among Euripides' later works of what he calls *mêchanêma* plots, in which the main characters are forced to take a desperate situation into their own hands and plot their salvation by means of intrigue (a similar pattern can be observed in, for example, *Helen, Iphigenia among the Taurians* and the fragmentary *Antiope*).[8] This type of pattern is clearly seen in *Orestes*. Other large-scale patterns have also been perceived as underlying the play. Anne Pippin Burnett, for example, argued that an Aristotelian approach could after all prove helpful for understanding *Orestes* and other supposedly ill-constructed Euripidean tragedies. According to Burnett, *Orestes* is structured around a principle of *peripeteia* ('reversal' – a concept which is central to Aristotle's discussion of plot in the *Poetics*). The plot moves

2. Dramatic Structure and Performance

forward, she explains, by a series of calculated reversals of expectation culminating in 'catastrophe survived'.[9]

Even if we do persist in finding the plot chaotic, we might choose to interpret chaos as a deliberate structural principle rather than a sign of faulty construction. This view is taken by Spira, Solmsen and other scholars, who see the world of *Orestes* as a terrifying, godless and unintelligible place, in which human actions are governed by *tychê* (chance or randomness).[10] The apparent lack of design in the events on stage could be seen as mirroring the lack of pattern in the world as a whole. Thus the play's structure, in the eyes of some, may in fact be a clue to its (deeply pessimistic) meaning: it is all about the difficulties of human life and morality in the face of a confusing and terrifying universe.

Whether or not we agree fully with any of these views, it seems too simple just to say that the plot of *Orestes* is badly put together. It is surely more likely that the play was deliberately constructed in order to create a particular effect. The effect on each individual spectator no doubt varied, but (as before) I suggest that the key to understanding both the plot and the performative aspects of *Orestes* is the 'incongruity factor'. In other words, not only were the events that took place in the play disconcertingly at odds with the audience's previous knowledge of the Orestes story (as we have seen in Chapter 1), but also – just as importantly – the unconventional manner in which these events were staged, and the appearance and sound of the play in performance, seem designed to startle the spectators.

Prologue (1-139)

Technically the term *prologos* refers to everything up to the first entrance of the chorus. Here the *prologos* is divided into two parts: Electra's monologue, followed by a scene of dialogue. At first, the stage is empty apart from Electra, who (as we have seen) seems to be addressing her words directly to the audience, and her brother Orestes, who is prostrate and silent on his sick-bed by the *skênê* (which represents the royal palace at Argos).

Euripides: Orestes

After Electra has completed her strangely ironical narrative of past events in her awful family (see Chapter 1), she reveals their current predicament. It is six days since Orestes murdered his mother, and the Furies have punished Orestes by afflicting him with a form of physically wasting mental illness. The people of Argos have already decreed that no one is to have any contact with Orestes or Electra, and on this day the assembly will vote on whether to pass sentence of death upon them. The siblings' only hope of rescue seems to be from their uncle Menelaus, who has arrived in force at Nauplia harbour, on the way home from the Trojan War.

All of this prepares the audience for Menelaus' imminent arrival on the scene (together with lines 67-9, in which Electra says she is looking down every road for his approach). But instead, a quite different character enters: Menelaus' wife, Helen (71). This is a highly effective instance of audience misdirection.[11] Helen's appearance is surprising, not just because it is an example of 'false preparation' but because it is strange for Helen of Troy to appear at all in a tragedy about Orestes. In no other treatment of the myth had the two branches of the family come together in this way: what role can Helen have to play in the events that follow? It is almost as if Helen and Menelaus have wandered in from the wrong tragedy.

Helen, who is ashamed to show her face in public, asks Electra to take a libation to the tomb of Clytemnestra on her behalf. Electra is reluctant to do this, but persuades Helen to send her daughter Hermione instead. Helen gives the grave-offerings, which include a lock of her hair, to Hermione (who remains mute) and they both exit. When Electra is alone, she again turns to the audience (128-9) and asks them: 'Did you see how she has preserved her beauty by cutting her hair only at the ends? – yes, she is the same old Helen.' She is still cursing Helen when the chorus finally enter.

The ancient commentator on the text tells us that producers in his day made this scene even more remarkable in terms of staging: the actor playing Helen was made to enter on a chariot laden with the spoils of Troy.[12] This is in line with what we know

2. Dramatic Structure and Performance

of audiences' tastes in the fourth century BC and later, when more props and increased use of spectacular effects (especially entrances and exits) were considered to be *de rigueur*. Scholars argue about the exact point at which Helen would have made her 'enhanced' entrance, since it would have involved a procession onto the stage. If such a procession was added *before* line 1, as many suspect, this would mean that the 'surprise' effect of 67-9 would have been spoiled (but perhaps the prologue was cut or altered in some other, additional way).

More recent productions have made more striking changes to this important, 'scene-setting' prologue and the first entries of the play's main characters. Jan Kott's 1968 version (at the University of California, Berkeley) made its political overtones extremely clear by exchanging the Argive setting for a version of contemporary Washington, DC, and projecting an enormous photographic image of the Capitol as the backdrop. Kott's production was notable for its overt 'anti-war' message: indeed, the director saw the main theme of the play as being 'madness and violence, both domestic and foreign ... so appropriate for our own times'.[13] His chorus came on stage carrying placards with slogans such as 'We're All Murderers', 'Get Out of Troy Now' and 'Helen is a Whore'.

By contrast, Helen Edmundson's 2006 adaptation of *Orestes* chose to emphasize its domestic and familial rather than its political aspects. The prologue of her version takes place in Clytemnestra's bedroom, and Orestes and Electra are both seen lying down, covered with blood, on Clytemnestra's double bed (which has connotations both of childbirth and of love-making). Helen's entry on the scene, resplendent in white evening-dress, provides (as in the original text) a striking contrast with the dirt and degradation of the siblings.[14]

Charles Mee's 1992 adaptation of the play (which has been restaged several times in different versions) opens with 'a matter-of-fact recitation of Clytemnestra's autopsy report' – a device which reproduces and cleverly updates the 'prologue-speech' convention.[15] Mee sets the play's events in the psychiatric ward of a hospital, emphasizing the theme of madness which runs so prominently through the play. His Orestes in this version is markedly insane throughout: in fact, many of the other characters are also called on to writhe madly around the stage, against a background of bandaged, bed-ridden and wheelchair-bound invalids. Meanwhile, Mee's Helen makes an entrance just as striking, in its way, as Euripides' original, speaking lines from cosmetics advertisements in *Vogue* magazine and other sources. As one reviewer noted, Mee's script is a 'paste-up', which 'mashes up Greek tragedy with texts culled from serial-killer testimonies, fashion magazines and astrology columns'.[16] This odd technique, which many have found baffling or alienating, is actually a highly effective means of bringing out the allusive and intertextual quality of Euripides' script.

Parodos (140-207)

The Argive women make a striking entrance – on tiptoe, so as to avoid waking Orestes. They sing in a rhythm dominated by dochmiacs (a metre often used to create tension). The chorus-leader's first words are an instruction to the other chorus members to keep silence (140), but Electra, who joins in the song, has to ask them to be even quieter (145-6), and later (181-2) reproves them for making a loud clatter.

The subject of the song is the pitiable sickness of Orestes: the singers congregate around his bed as they lament his sufferings. Electra several times questions the behaviour of Apollo, who instructed Orestes to carry out the murder. When it seems that Orestes is soundly asleep, Electra sings a hymn to 'mistress Night, giver of sleep' (174-5).

The *parodos* establishes the close relationship between Electra and the women of the chorus, who are clearly sympathetic to the siblings in their ordeal. Even though the scene is, conventionally, played out of doors, a sense of intimacy is created: the audience is made to feel that they are watching a scene of a private, domestic (and, indeed, rather squalid) sort. The musical style of the *parodos* is typical of later Euripides, in that it

2. Dramatic Structure and Performance

takes the form of a lyric duet (*amoibaion*) between the chorus and the solo singer who played the part of Electra.[17] There are other touches of the 'New Musical' style in these lyrics, including the loose syntax, the repetitious word-setting, the fluid use of metre, and the use of voices to imitate the pan-pipe (*syrinx*).[18] (I return to the 'New Music' in Chapter 4 below.)

The chorus is probably the most difficult aspect of any Greek tragedy to stage in the modern theatre. Even in the case of *Orestes*, where we are lucky enough to possess a small amount of the play's original musical notation (see below), it is virtually impossible to know just how the songs sounded. Many modern productions reduce the role of the chorus, or require the actors to chant their lines in unison, in a kind of 'choral speaking' (which gives a misleading impression of the function of the chorus, and is often rather deadening for the audience). Other recent adaptations cut out the chorus altogether: for example, Charles Mee's *Orestes*, mentioned above, dispenses with a chorus but includes eclectic 'soundtrack' music by Irving Berlin, The Jackson Five and others, for the purpose of providing interludes between scenes.[19] Edmundson's adaptation, on similar lines, reduced the chorus to a solitary 'Slave' figure.

Even those directors who are brave enough to retain the chorus in a musical role, and who are able to commission a new score from a composer, run the risk of failing to create the required tone: a production of *Orestes* in 2006 by Classic Greek Theatre of Oregon was criticized for its 'silly, dance-hall choreography' and chorus who 'sound at times like a lesbian folk collective'.[20] Another production (directed by Kate Bosher of the University of Toronto in 1994) was criticized for the confusing shifts in tone – a mixture of 'solemn grief' and 'grinning foolishness' – which the chorus created.[21] No doubt Euripides himself is responsible for many of these perceived shifts in tone; but it will be clear enough that there are difficulties in store for any modern director who wants to put a chorus on stage.

Euripides: Orestes

Dialogue between Electra and Orestes (208-315)

The scene begins with a moment of terrible anxiety, which again challenges the audience's expectations: Orestes is so soundly asleep that the chorus-leader believes that he has died (209-10). However (after, one presumes, a suitably long pause, to prolong the suspense), Orestes wakes up and groggily addresses his sister, who comforts and nurses him. At first Orestes speaks lucidly, but later (253ff.) he becomes disturbed and hallucinates. He imagines that Electra is one of the Furies, trying to cast him down into hell (264-5), and then has an imaginary fight using an invisible bow from Apollo (268-76). Eventually Orestes regains sanity and calm, and comforts his sister, reminding her that he alone was responsible for the murder and urging her to take rest. Electra returns into the house, and Orestes lies down again on his bed.

Most unusually, we happen to know the name of the actor who played the role of Orestes in the original production: he was called Hegelochus. This information is preserved purely because of an embarrassing mistake which Hegelochus made during this scene. At line 279, when Orestes has recovered from his fit of insanity, he says: 'I can see the calm after the storm'. But in Greek the word 'calm' (*galén*) sounds very similar to the word 'weasel' (*galê*). Hegelochus got the accent wrong, and thus what the audience heard was: 'I can see the weasel after the storm.' The actor never lived it down: comedians years later were still making fun of his pronunciation.[22]

Choral song (316-47)

The chorus' first word is *aiai* (316), an untranslatable cry of anguish and despair. In this short, unhappy act-dividing song they beseech the Furies to leave Orestes alone, and lament the sufferings of the family, reflecting that prosperity does not endure among men (340-3). As in the *parodos*, the metre is predominantly dochmiac, appropriate to the mood of tension and foreboding. One of the most remarkable things about this

2. Dramatic Structure and Performance

song is that the original musical notation is partially preserved.[23] The melody, written in the Phrygian mode, was designed to be accompanied on the shawm.

Second act (348-806)

As the chorus finish singing and dancing, Menelaus at last makes his long-anticipated entry. The lines which imply that he entered in considerable pomp and finery (349-51) may be the work of a later producer or actor who wanted to create a more spectacular visual effect in performance (we may compare the scholiast's comment on Helen's entry at line 57, mentioned above).[24] But if the lines are genuine Menelaus' costume and trappings would have made an effective, significant contrast with the scruffy, awful appearance of Orestes, which is remarked upon at some length (385-91). It also strikes me that any mention of Menelaus' smart appearance here might have seemed particularly pointed to anyone in the audience who remembered Euripides' *Helen* (in which Menelaus was so dirty and ragged that he was unrecognizable to his wife). Our suspicions that this may be yet another example of Euripidean self-consciousness are increased when we also recall that Aristophanes ridiculed Euripides for his penchant for portraying heroes in rags.[25]

Menelaus questions Orestes, in an unusually lengthy sequence of stichomythia (385-447), about what has been happening to him. But as the scene progresses, it becomes less likely that Menelaus' arrival will actually result in the longed-for deliverance that it promised. At 456 a new threat presents itself, in the form of Tyndareus, Menelaus' father-in-law. The old man staggers onto the stage, assisted by mute attendants (whom he addresses at 629): he is dressed in dark mourning costume and has cut off his hair, in remembrance of his daughter Clytemnestra (457-8). He greets Menelaus before catching sight of the 'mother-murdering serpent' Orestes (479), who arouses his anger.

What follows, without any announcement, is a set-piece scene of a type which Euripides and Sophocles particularly

Euripides: Orestes

favoured, especially in their later plays: that is, an *agôn* or courtroom-style debate between Tyndareus and Orestes.[26] Tyndareus begins by putting the 'case for the prosecution' and Orestes responds with the 'defence'. The *agôn* does not succeed in establishing Orestes' guilt or innocence: it merely explores the background and moral implications of the crime from a number of different angles. As usual in scenes of this type, the audience is left to make up its own mind, and the action of the play continues as if the debate had not taken place (in stark contrast to the famous courtroom scene in Aeschylus' *Eumenides*, which debates the same case but does result in a verdict and a clear outcome). The staging of this and other *agôn*-scenes poses unanswerable questions. It is hard to say how far (if at all) the visual presentation, body-language and acting style here would have reflected the sudden change of register, and equally hard to say what degree of 'realism' one should expect. But it is clear that the *agôn* constituted a 'pause' in the plot – a distinct scene-within-a-scene, marked off rather artificially from the play's action proper.

Following this inconclusive debate, Tyndareus resolves to stir up the Argives in hatred of Orestes and Electra; he also warns Menelaus against helping the siblings. Following his exit (629), Menelaus visibly loses his resolve and starts to dither as he looks for a way of getting out of his responsibilities. Orestes supplicates him at length, in what turns out to be almost a second *agôn* (640-717), since Menelaus is forced to make a long answering speech. Menelaus exits, having made what seems an ineffectual promise to try to win over the Argive assembly (717). By a neat but unlikely coincidence (of a type which is common in tragedy), at the very moment that this 'worst of friends' (719) has departed the stage, Orestes sees Pylades, his 'dearest of friends' (725), approaching. Another long scene of increasingly rapid-fire dialogue (*stichomythia*, 734-73, followed by *antilabê*, 774-98) establishes Pylades' credentials as a friend: he will support Orestes and Electra, even if he ends up suffering for it. The scene ends with the symbolic image of Orestes leaning on

2. Dramatic Structure and Performance

his friend as he leaves the stage (*en route* for the tomb of Agamemnon, where he will pray for good fortune). This scene is interesting not just because of the stylized *agôn* (however it is staged), but because it is the first scene in the play in which we see an on-stage conflict between major characters who are opposed to one another in temperament. In Albert Weiner's 1969 staging (at the State University of New York, Albany), this opposition – conceived of in terms of a 'generation gap' between the younger and older characters – was exploited in the play's staging, which was arranged on two levels. Orestes, Electra and Pylades (represented as drab, ragged figures with no make-up) occupied the main area of the stage, while Menelaus and Tyndareus (in rich, elaborate costumes) hovered above them on a giant theatrical boot (*kothornos*). No contact was possible between the two levels – a form of staging which emphasized the lack of common ground and empathy between the characters.[27]

Choral song (807-43)

This unexpectedly morose and pessimistic ode contrasts with the relatively up-beat ending of the previous scene. The chorus sing, as they did before, of the matricide, the sufferings of Orestes, and the fall of the house of Atreus. They trace back the misfortunes of the family to Thyestes' and Atreus' dispute over the golden lamb (a dispute which Electra mentioned in the prologue). But the point of this ode is not simply descriptive. As well as lamenting the current wretched state of the royal family, the chorus also introduce a note of sophistic paradox, as they sing (819-24) of 'a non-good good deed' (*to kalon ou kalon*), 'right wrongdoing' (*to d' eu kakourgein*) and 'fancy sin' (*asebeia poikila*). The language and meaning in the closing antistrophe are so obscure that textual corruption has been suspected,[28] but at any rate it seems clear that the chorus' presentation of the moral rights and wrongs of the case is designed to be peculiar and provocative.

Euripides: Orestes

Third act (844-959)

Electra emerges from the house and is struck by her brother's absence. The chorus-leader tells her that he has gone to face the Argive assembly. Electra starts to question the chorus-leader, but a messenger arrives to report that the assembly has passed sentence of death. This decision is seen as the outcome of a deeply flawed debate: the assembly is described as a rowdy mob, split by faction and swayed by speakers whose motives are questionable, self-interested or malignant. The messenger tells Electra that Orestes and Pylades are on their way back to the palace in tears, accompanied by their supporters (950: an odd detail, since these 'friends' are not in evidence at any other point in the play – is it a continuity error?). The scene ends with the news that Orestes and Electra will not, as feared, meet their death by public stoning, but that they will have to commit suicide before the day is out.

Choral song (960-1012)

The chorus respond to the terrible news by singing another *kommos*, this time accompanied by all the traditional gestures of a ritual lament: they wail aloud, they scratch their faces so as to draw blood, they beat their chests and heads.[29] West comments, suggestively, that if this were an Aeschylean tragedy it might have ended at this point.[30] Electra once again joins in the singing, expressing a wish to soar up into space, where Tantalus resides in perpetual suspension amid heavenly objects and cosmic whirlwinds: her weirdly 'cosmologized' escape-fantasy echoes the earlier description of Tantalus (in the prologue, 4-10). All the singers here emphasize again the unpredictability of human life and fortunes (976-81), and the decisive final word of the song is 'necessity' (*anankais*, 1012).

Fourth act (1013-1245)

Orestes and Pylades return, and the plot thickens. From this point to the end of the play, the structure becomes freer and

2. Dramatic Structure and Performance

more elaborate, with a mixture of shorter scenes divided by brief choral interludes. This episode starts with Orestes' and Electra's emotional meeting and tearful embrace. They are beginning to come to terms with their imminent death, and are asking their friend to take charge of the arrangements for their burial, when Pylades interrupts. His shout of 'Stop!' (1069) can be seen as the turning-point in the play's two-part structure – the moment at which Orestes and Electra become actively involved in altering their own fate, rather than passive victims of circumstance.

However, it is Pylades who is really in charge now: this is a quite remarkable transformation of his role (both in this play and in the mythical tradition generally). Hitherto, and in Aeschylus and Sophocles, Pylades has been a minor – or even mute – character, a 'foil' to Orestes; now he has become the driving force behind the play's increasingly strange plot developments. We are even told (somewhat implausibly, and in contradiction to other versions) that it was Pylades who devised the unspecified 'atrocities' (1158) suffered by Clytemnestra's lover Aegisthus before the start of the play. Pylades says: 'Since we are about to die, let us hatch a plan together, so that Menelaus may suffer too' (1098-9). He outlines a sordid plot to murder Helen and burn down the palace, to which Orestes responds enthusiastically.

A further twist follows, for Electra now adds another suggestion, which is applauded by Pylades and Orestes (1177ff.): perhaps they might escape altogether, if they can kidnap Hermione and use her as a hostage to prevent Menelaus from harming them. 'And in fact I think she is approaching the house even now,' says Electra; 'why, the very length of time corresponds nicely' (1214-15). These lines amount to a self-conscious reference to the tragedians' habit (noted above) of including overly convenient 'coincidences' in their plots. Willink, in his commentary, rightly emphasizes Euripides' audacity in drawing attention to this convention ('almost challenging the spectator to notice the *incongruity* of time'), coupled with the fact that Hermione does *not* actually enter for another hundred lines or so.[31]

Euripides: Orestes

Amoibaion (1246-1310)

Electra and the women of the chorus remain outside to keep watch, while Orestes and Pylades enter through the *skênê* doors: the scene is set for murder. Meanwhile Electra joins the chorus for another segment of dialogue in sung lyrics. The chorus members divide themselves into two semichoruses, one guarding each *eisodos* in case of intruders or onlookers. (The increased number of singers and the division of parts means that the attribution of lines becomes more difficult – Greek manuscripts seldom indicate a change of speaker – and consequently modern editions may differ from each other at this point.)

At 1269-70 the chorus announce that someone – an anonymous 'hunter' – can be seen moving about near the palace. This creates the false expectation that this unknown character will burst on the scene, but in fact no one appears at all. This variation on the technique of 'false preparation' (cf. 67-71, 1366-9) is perhaps rather strange, but it contributes to the overall mood of tension and expectation which characterizes the scene. Can it really be that Helen will be murdered? That would constitute an outrageous reversal of the mythical tradition (not that Euripides was averse to altering myths – as seen in his previous tragedy *Helen*, which also reversed certain details of Helen's story).[32]

As if impatient at the slowness of her co-conspirators, Electra puts her ear to the closed doors of the *skênê* and shouts encouragement through the panels (1284): 'You inside! What are you waiting for?'[33] Almost at once we hear Helen screaming: 'Alas! Pelasgian Argos! I am dying utterly!' (1296); and 'Menelaus! I am perishing, and you are not present to help me!' (1301). These sound exactly like conventional death-cries,[34] and so the audience will naturally infer – for the time being – that Helen is dead.

Hermione is tricked (1311-52)

Electra spies Hermione approaching and tells the chorus to stop shouting: clearly their last song was a very loud one (1314; cf.

2. Dramatic Structure and Performance

1325). Hermione asks Electra to explain the commotion, and Electra says that everyone has been lamenting her own and Orestes' death-sentence. The gullible Hermione agrees to go and join the others, who she believes are inside, begging Helen for help. As she is on the point of entering the *skênê*, she is seized by Menelaus and Orestes (1347-52). Electra urges her brother to press his sword to her throat, and so show Menelaus that he is dealing with 'proper men, not cowardly Phrygians' (1351-2) – lines which will come to seem ironic in the light of what follows at 1369.

Choral song (1353-65)

A very brief strophic interlude. (It will be answered by another strophic song which uses the same metre and music, but this does not come until 1537.) Like the previous sung duet (1246-1310), this song is unusually loud and ferocious in nature, involving foot-stamping and shouting (1353). The chorus members proclaim that they want to distract attention from the events in the house, in case some one should hear and rush to Helen's aid – so, in other words, it is not absolutely clear whether or not Helen is dead. The effect of this uncertainty is puzzling and frustrating.

The singing and dancing breaks off when the chorus-leader hears the bars of the *skênê* doors creaking (1366-8) ...

The Phrygian's scene (1366-1536)

... but nothing could have prepared us for the bizarre scene that follows. We have been led to expect that the doors will swing open to reveal Helen's corpse on the *ekkyklêma*, but this turns out to have been yet another skilful piece of misdirection. Instead, the 'wrong' character appears, from the 'wrong' part of the stage, and behaves in a most unexpected way: it is a Phrygian slave who appears on the roof, descends to the *orchêstra*, and bursts into song.

This is one of the most astonishing entrances in Greek tragedy. The ancient commentators on this scene reflect the extraordinariness of the scene when they suggest that the actor entered the stage by jumping off the *skênê* roof. Modern scholars have doubted whether this would have been physically possible (how tall was the *skênê*?); but the use of the *mêchanê* would have enabled an air-borne entry to be made without any risk to the actor.[35] The *mêchanê* would also have added another (entirely appropriate) layer of incongruity, particularly since in tragedy the device was not normally used for human characters.

Everything about this scene is out of the ordinary. By this stage, like Electra and the chorus, we are desperate to find out what has happened to Helen: we do not expect to see the action delayed yet further, by what turns out to be the longest monody in any tragedy. We do not expect an anonymous, servile, barbarian character to have such a prominent role, and we certainly do not expect him to sing an elaborate 'operatic' aria in place of a more conventional iambic messenger-speech. The musical style in which the aria is composed is (as before) jarringly modern, full of 'New Musical' touches such as repetition, the miscellaneous juxtaposition of different metres, and the subordination of meaning to musical and onomatopoeic sound-effects. Indeed, whether because of the 'New Musical' style or because of the barbarian's poor command of Greek, it is hard to tell what he is actually singing about. The chorus-leader implores the Phrygian: 'Tell us *plainly* what happened in the house' (1393) – but to no avail.

The hazy picture which eventually emerges from the Phrygian's song is of a scene of utter carnage and chaos. It appears that all Helen's attendants (apart from the singer) have been slain by Orestes and Pylades, and it is strongly implied (at least) that Helen herself is dead,[36] but the obfuscatory manner of narration seems designed to leave the audience in the dark as regards precise details. Euripides, it seems, wants to prolong our uncertainty: it is crucial that we do *not* learn at this stage all that has happened. This effect would be much harder to achieve with a 'normal' messenger-speech.

Critics argue about how *funny* the Phrygian and his aria are

2. Dramatic Structure and Performance

meant to be. Many have found the character completely ridiculous – an overwrought, gibberish-spouting barbarian of a type that would be more at home in comedy than tragedy.[37] (The reader is warned that many modern translations over-emphasize the silliness and incomprehensibility of the Phrygian's Greek.[38]) Nevertheless, the slave's barbarism and clownishness is much less marked than the typical foreigners of Aristophanic drama (the Scythian archer in *Women at the Thesmophoria*, the Triballian god in *Birds*, and so on), and in fact he speaks recognizably Attic Greek (allowing for the distortions of lyric language and the 'New Musical' style) rather than the mangled Greek of comic barbarians. This character is certainly incongruous, even grotesque – but that is not the same as 'comic'.

Of the lines of dialogue that follow (1503-36), West remarks: 'There is no funnier scene in Greek tragedy.' Some critics have been so troubled by the presence of a funny scene in tragedy that they have been tempted to delete the lines entirely.[39] But tragedy does from time to time contain lighter moments, which contribute to the overall design by introducing moments of contrast and tension;[40] and the lines here do not seem out of place with the mood of the play as a whole. As the Phrygian comes to the end of his song, Orestes comes out of the *skênê* doors, sword in hand (1504), and asks the cowering slave a series of threatening questions, which include a number of rather menacing 'jokes'. Orestes eventually spares the Phrygian so that he can go off and fetch Menelaus. Orestes returns through the *skênê* doors; the Phrygian exits by one of the *eisodoi*.

One of the first traceable performances of *Orestes* in modern times was Richard Valpy's production at Reading School in 1821.[41] It seems, from contemporary accounts of this production, that Dr Valpy favoured rather extreme methods for getting the best results from his actors. In order to produce a convincing effect of 'distraught panic, abject terror and crouching humility' from B.B. Bockett, the boy actor who played the Phrygian, Valpy would beat him just before his entrance onto the stage!

Euripides: Orestes

Choral song (1537-48)

Another brief interlude, answering the earlier strophe at 1353-65 and using the same music. As Willink points out in his commentary, this 'long-range responsion' in effect marks off lines 1353-1548 as a self-contained act-within-an-act. The chorus sing yet again of the fall of the house of Atreus. As they sing, they notice smoke rising from the front of the palace (1542). Their final utterance begins: 'The house is falling, is falling!' (1547) – a common enough image in tragedy, which here is transformed into a real threat, as it seems that the house may *literally* be destroyed.

Final act and *deus ex machina* (1549-1693)

As the *dénouement* approaches, the stage becomes much busier. First of all, Menelaus approaches with a large crowd of 'extras', who represent his armed forces along with members of the Argive public. Once again, the audience's attention is drawn to the 'wrong' part of the stage: Menelaus orders his soldiers to break down the palace doors, but immediately the other characters appear on top of the *skênê*.[42] Orestes has his sword to Hermione's throat, while Pylades is holding blazing torches. This is the only tragedy to culminate in a roof-top hostage scenario – an unusually exciting scene, which is also impressive in visual and theatrical terms.

The number of speaking characters in this scene (Orestes, Menelaus and, later, Apollo) means that the roles of Pylades and Hermione must now be played by mute actors. Euripides, in a typically self-conscious gesture, even draws particular attention to this fact. When Menelaus asks Pylades if he will be personally involved in Hermione's killing, Orestes replies for him (1592): 'He says yes silently; it will suffice for me to do the talking.' With this bizarre line Euripides is not merely alluding to the three-actor technique; he is perhaps also making intertextual play with the notorious scene in Aeschylus' *Libation-Bearers* where the mute Pylades unexpectedly speaks a line.[43]

2. Dramatic Structure and Performance

Orestes threatens (1567-72) to tear the house apart with his bare hands and throw pieces of masonry down onto Menelaus – another clear sign that the house of Atreus is facing literal and symbolic 'ruin'. There follows a long scene of rapid dialogue (*stichomythia* combined with *antilabê*, 1576-1618) between Orestes and Menelaus, in which Orestes makes his demands: unless Menelaus leaves him alone to rule Argos as king, he will kill Hermione and set fire to the palace. Just at the point when Menelaus has lost patience and is urging the Argives to storm the palace, Apollo appears, with Helen, on the *mêchanê* (1625). Thus, as West observes, we are presented with 'a spectacular tableau on four levels, unique in ancient drama' – the *orchêstra*, the front of the *skênê*, the roof, and the *mêchanê* on high are all full of activity.

Euripides seems to have been particularly fond of rounding off his plays' action with a *deus ex machina* (the device is seen also in *Andromache, Bacchae, Electra, Hippolytus, Suppliant Women, Iphigenia among the Taurians, Helen, Ion* and *Rhesus*), but such scenes have often been thought to be artificial, unrealistic or otherwise unsatisfactory.[44] Here Apollo's speech clears up the mystery of Helen's 'death' and settles the fate of all the other main characters, in a speech which has struck many critics as problematic or even absurd.[45]

There was no curtain in Greek tragedy, which means that the exact moment at which the play finished would have been hard to identify. The crowd will have dispersed gradually, and all the other characters will have had to make their exits from the various parts of the stage, followed by the chorus. The last lines of the play in our transmitted texts (1691-3) consist of a few sung verses in anapaestic rhythm, in which the chorus pray to the goddess Nike (Victory) that the play might win the contest. These feeble, 'illusion-breaking' lines, which also appear at the end of other tragedies in the manuscript tradition (e.g. *Iphigenia among the Taurians* and *Phoenician Women*), are probably spurious.

Modern adaptations of *Orestes* have tended to interpret the *deus ex machina* scene as a particularly striking moment within

Euripides: Orestes

the play: all of them, significantly, seem to have brought out its more ironical or outrageous aspects. For instance, in Albert Weiner's New York production (see above), Apollo did not appear in person, but his presence was represented by a powerful burst of 'sunshine' on the cyclorama, while an actor read out his speech through loudspeakers in a deliberately tentative, drunken tone of voice: 'And Orestes shall marry ... er ... Hermione.' Meanwhile streamers and balloons floated down from the ceiling as the actors sung 'Auld Lang Syne'.[46] The seemingly arbitrary and unsatisfactory nature of the ending is also emphasized in Mee's *Orestes*, in which Apollo makes his final appearance as a TV quiz show host, dispensing the 'prizes' from a number of television sets arranged around the stage. However, in other productions of Mee's adaptation, Apollo has been put on stage in the guise of the current American president,[47] or, alternatively, as an electronic robot which malfunctions and has to be carried off.[48] Nancy Meckler's recent staging of Edmundson's *Orestes* sticks closer to Euripides, but still emphasizes the absurdity of the ending, displaying Apollo on a giant see-saw.[49]

It is clear that scholars, directors and audiences alike have found the ending the most difficult part of the play to swallow, despite its great potential for dazzling spectacle. Can we take it seriously? Who can say whether or not true 'closure' has been achieved? As with so much else in this play, it is hard to decide just what this ending means. Nevertheless, we shall discuss the play's ending, along with its treatment of Apollo, in more detail in the next chapter.

3

Humans and Gods

In this chapter I look at the characters who take part in the play's action, and examine their behaviour both in relation to one another and in relation to the supernatural forces which govern the universe. The history of this doomed family involves shocking violations of normal behaviour – adultery, cannibalism and murder, all within a closed circle of relatives – and our natural reaction may well be one of revulsion or horror. Yet at the same time we tend to feel a measure of sympathy for the characters. This conflicting mixture of responses may explain why the story of Orestes has such an enduring appeal as a myth and as a subject for tragedy. Orestes, Agamemnon, Clytemnestra and the others are not simply monsters, but credible human beings with whom we can identify to some extent.

Many scholarly studies of *Orestes* (and the other tragedies dealing with the same myth) focus on evaluating the central characters' behaviour from an ethical perspective. Was Orestes right to act as he did? Does he deserve to be punished? Did Clytemnestra deserve to die? Was she justified in murdering Agamemnon? Is it ever right to kill members of one's own family? Do the gods care? Such questions of guilt or innocence are bound to arise whenever we read the play.

In a sense, these ethical questions are of universal relevance. It is amazing that, despite the huge cultural differences that exist between our world and that of the characters, we can still respond with such intensity to the tragic myth. All the same, its apparent familiarity and easy comprehensibility should not make us ignore the gap in space and time. It can be tempting to interpret the myth with reference to 'human nature' as a whole,

Euripides: Orestes

but in fact modern views of character and personality are very different from ancient views.[1] As always, of course, we are free to make of the plays whatever we wish – but, as a starting-point, it is worth making an effort to understand how Euripides' original audience would have seen these characters. The issues which are central to understanding the characters – heredity, reciprocity, familial love, revenge, guilt, and so on – are not simply universal principles but have a culturally specific significance.

In particular, the fifth-century Greeks would have found it hard to conceive of such matters as character, motivation, responsibility, or normal or abnormal states of mind on a purely human level, without reference to the gods. This is probably the main difference between ancient and modern approaches to character, and it suggests that we should probably not try to interpret *Orestes* as a 'psychological drama' in the modern sense. The human action is always to be interpreted in the light of superhuman powers.

The characters

The writer of one of the *hypotheses* (the ancient plot-summaries transmitted along with the plays in manuscript) concluded his account of *Orestes* by declaring that all its characters, with the exception of Pylades, are rotten (*phauloi*). This is a somewhat simplistic and insensitive judgement (and, in general, the quality of scholarship in these *hypotheses* is distinctly patchy),[2] but many subsequent readers have more or less agreed with it.[3] It seems to me that Euripides' characterization is actually far more subtle than this black-and-white image implies. Euripides could have chosen to present these characters as unmitigated rotters or villains, but instead he has chosen to depict them in a more ambiguous way, giving them both positive and negative attributes. This technique would have evoked contradictory feelings in the audience, making it difficult or impossible for them to evaluate the characters. But this is entirely appropriate, perhaps, in a play where nothing at all is easy to interpret.

A crucial factor when considering 'characterization' is that

3. Humans and Gods

Euripides and the other tragedians, unlike most modern playwrights and novelists, did not invent their characters: as we have seen, they inherited them from the mythical tradition. Before they went to see *Orestes,* the audience already knew – or believed they knew – the characters, because they had encountered them so many times before in drama and other forms of mythical narrative. This is why, as Aristotle wrote, it would have been impossible to write a tragedy in which (for instance) Orestes did *not* kill Clytemnestra (*Poetics* 1453b22-6). But that still left considerable scope for variety in the precise manner in which the characters talked, explained their motivation, and conducted themselves on stage. Indeed, the tragedians often seem to be prompting their audiences to re-evaluate characters whom they thought they understood.

Playwrights tended to use the same characters repeatedly, and it is particularly interesting to compare and contrast the use of characters in different plays by the same playwright. For instance, we respond to the Orestes of *Orestes* in part because he is different from the Orestes of *Electra* or *Iphigenia among the Taurians.* In fact, versions of all the major characters in *Orestes* also appear in other Euripidean tragedies, and they strike us as significantly different in each case.

Electra, the first character whom we encounter, initially seems very different from the title character of Euripides' *Electra* (probably produced within about five years of *Orestes*), who married a peasant and pretended to have given birth to his son in order to lure Clytemnestra to her death. She is also more calm and rational than the highly-wrought Electra of Sophocles' *Electra*, who has struck many readers as being insane. As we have already noted, Electra's odd detachment and 'illusion-breaking' addresses to the audience (1-70, 128-9) may seem to mark her out as a different type of character altogether, one who never *quite* manages to convince us that she is real. But like these other Electras, she is preoccupied throughout the play with suffering – her own and that of the other characters – and she is given to lamentation (e.g. 194-207, 982-1017). Her love and devotion to Orestes is seen from the start, as she tends him in his sickness, and it continues unwaveringly throughout the play. When it becomes clear that the siblings must die by their own hand, Electra cries out in agony, and even hints that she is starting to lose her mind (1020-1). Orestes, showing manly reserve, initially tells her to be quiet (1022-32), but soon softens and embraces her (1045-51).

Until this point Electra has played a largely subordinate or passive part in events (a part which will be familiar from Aeschylus and Sophocles), but now she seems to gain in authority. It is she, not Orestes or Pylades, who is responsible for the plot to kidnap and violate Hermione (1176-1203). It has even been thought that Electra's plan springs from a 'hideous malice' against the young Hermione, and that at its root lies the sexual jealousy of an old maid; but, if so, one would perhaps expect Euripides to have emphasized this aspect more in the text.[4] The real significance of Electra's active plotting is not so much that it reveals her 'ulterior motives' but that it emphasizes the equal status and solidarity of the three desperadoes.

Another significance of Electra's increasingly active role in the plot can be seen in comparison to Euripides' other 'Electra', the heroine of *Electra*, who was the driving force behind the revenge plot in that play. Indeed, Electra can be compared more generally to other powerful female characters in Euripides (such as Helen, Iphigenia, and Medea) who take control of the action in their respective situations, and who have often struck readers or viewers as being markedly superior to their counterpart male characters in practical and intellectual terms.[5]

Orestes himself has struck many readers as being utterly terrible – 'a matricidal monster' – 'base and inhuman' – 'wrong-headed and weak' – 'disgusting' (to quote just a few representative epithets).[6] True, he has committed atrocious deeds, and his attempts at self-justification can seem misguided or amoral, as when (in his *agôn* with Tyndareus, 544-604) he claims to be a benefactor of all mankind, or when he claims that Menelaus 'owes' him a murder (655: see below). Even if Orestes seems to win our sympathy in the first half of the play, when he is apparently racked by remorse and pitifully weakened by

3. Humans and Gods

disease, it may be that he forfeits it with his reckless behaviour during the second half.[7] The murder-plot in *Orestes* casts a new light on the previous murders, because it shows that Orestes is the type of person who will kill, not just in the specific and unique situation of avenging his father, but in a totally different situation too, in order to save his own skin. Perhaps he is simply meant to strike the audience as the sort of person to whom murder comes naturally.

But on the other hand, we can take a more positive view of Orestes' character. Euripides stresses repeatedly that the matricide was carried out under the influence of Apollo, and that Orestes believed he was acting rightly (e.g. 28-32, 268-70, 275-6, 285-7). Even if we disapprove of the killing of Helen, it is hard to find lines that can be taken as evidence of Orestes' inherently evil nature. Perhaps Orestes did what anyone else would do in the circumstances. One recent interpretation argues that the play is really 'a study in victimization', showing the lengths to which one may be driven by a cruel, unjust, malevolent world. Should we see Orestes primarily as a *victim* rather than a criminal?[8] Whatever our answer to that question, it is again worth considering other portrayals of Orestes. It seems to me that Orestes in this play is portrayed much more sympathetically than in Euripides' *Electra*, and he is almost certainly less evil than the cold-blooded, emotionless Orestes of Sophocles' *Electra*, whom one scholar described as a 'killing machine'.[9]

This Orestes is not driven into exile and hounded from place to place by the Erinyes (as he was in other tragedies), but he has been made physically ill by them. Euripides' description of Orestes' squalid, emaciated state is gruesome: he lies, unwashed, on filthy sheets, unable to move (39-42); he cannot eat (41, 189); he looks like a corpse (208-10, 385); his eyes and expression are hollow and wasted (389); he foams and dribbles at the mouth (219-20). He is also given to temporary fits of insanity, as we witness in a memorable scene towards the beginning of the play (253-76). His appearance changes and he becomes visibly agitated, thinking that the Erinyes are dragging him down into hell by the waist (264-5); he imagines that

Euripides: Orestes

he is fighting them off with an imaginary bow (268-74). This portrayal of sickness is unusually detailed and naturalistic: it has even been suggested that Euripides had some knowledge of Hippocratic medicine.[10]

We may compare this description with the very similar Orestes of *Iphigenia among the Taurians*, who is also driven insane by the Erinyes: the physical 'symptoms' (hallucination, raving, foaming at the mouth) are almost identical in each case. But Karelisa Hartigan has made an interesting comparison between Orestes and another mad Euripidean character – Heracles.[11] Both suffer a mixture of physical and mental symptoms, both fight with a (real or imagined) bow and arrows, and both mention the unusual Greek word *sunesis* in connection with their sufferings.[12] But whereas Heracles uses *sunesis* to mean 'understanding' or 'good sense', Orestes seems to mean something different by the word. When Menelaus asks him what sickness is afflicting him, Orestes answers: 'It is *sunesis* – that is, I am conscious of having done terrible crimes' (395-6). This line has prompted much discussion among scholars, many of whom see in it echoes of modern ideas of 'conscience' or even the 'subconscious'.[13] The difficulty lies partly in the translation of the key word, *sunesis*: Willink translates it as 'awareness', while West sees it as 'intellect', connected to Orestes' sense of guilt.

One must beware of reading too much 'psychology' into this scene; but all the same, Orestes' words are undoubtedly important, because (for their time) they seem to encapsulate a strikingly new and unusual way of thinking. Orestes is not talking about what we would now call the 'subconscious' as such, but this description of his mental processes does at least belong to an early stage in the development of the concept of an ethical consciousness or inner morality. Similar ideas seem to underlie a number of other fifth-century texts of various types, though it is not possible to reconstruct these ideas properly from such small glimpses as remain.[14] Nevertheless, it is clear that this Orestes is expressing himself in a way that would have been unthinkable for an earlier Orestes, and that Euripides has

3. Humans and Gods

to be interpreted in relation to his contemporary context of intellectual speculation (as in numerous other respects – see Chapter 6 below).

Why **Pylades** should be seen as exempt from the ancient scholar's charge of 'rottenness' is unclear. Like the other characters, he seems to embody a mixture of positive and negative qualities. His central characteristic, both here and elsewhere, is his loyal friendship with Orestes; but even this relationship is not entirely straightforward. We can choose to interpret it in a positive light, as a delightfully warm, genuinely touching human bond which contrasts with their unsatisfactory familial relationships. On the other hand, it is possible to talk not of friendship but of *folie à deux*, and many have seen the 'friends' as a couple of dangerous criminals, egging each other on to commit atrocious acts (especially in the murder-and-kidnap plot, 1100ff., but stress is also laid on Pylades' joint responsibility for Clytemnestra's murder: 767, 1089).

The most interesting aspect of Pylades' characterization in this play is that he is a major speaking character (rather than a minor character or a mute, as elsewhere in tragedy). He also exerts a powerful controlling influence over events. It is he who suggests the murder of Helen (1105), and he who, more chillingly, devised the (unspecified) 'atrocities' for Aegisthus (1158). At one point (883) his influence over Orestes is described as being like that of a tutor (*paidagôgos*) over a schoolboy – a striking image, perhaps recalling the sinister *paidagôgos* who manipulates Orestes in Sophocles' *Electra*. Pylades' character, and the young men's relationship, may assume a still more pejorative sense if we detect an underlying political significance (see Chapter 5 below).

The most ambiguous character of all is **Helen**, largely because of the contrast between the 'same old Helen' of this play (129) and the startlingly 'new' Helen of Euripides' *Helen* four years earlier (who did not elope with Paris or cause the Trojan War). This contrast between the two different 'Helens' is crucial to our understanding of the play (as we shall see again in the chapters which follow), since in *Orestes* Euripides frequently seems to be recalling the plot and themes of his *Helen*. Indeed, Euripides often returned (especially in his later plays) to the elusive and difficult-to-evaluate figure of Helen, who was so beautiful and beguiling and yet seemed to have been the cause of so much trouble in the world.[15] In this play, Euripides *seems* to be giving us the traditional Helen of myth; but the possibility of an *innocent*, likeable Helen is a disturbing one, not just because it would cause us to re-evaluate the events of the past, but because she herself is now a potential murder victim. It really *matters* whether we see Helen as good or evil – especially if we are trying to decide whether Orestes is justified in killing her – but Euripides makes it impossible to decide.[16] Some critics see her as vain, luxurious, and lacking in remorse; others see her as a rather 'charming' creature.[17] Our difficulties are increased by the fact that Helen does not appear on stage for long. In her scene of dialogue with Electra (71-125), she behaves decently but unremarkably, observing due respect for ritual and lamenting the miseries of the household. Her characterization is achieved largely through what the other characters say about her (e.g. 126-31, 520-2, 542-3, 737, 1131-42) – words which may or may not be true. But, whatever our view of Helen's behaviour, it is made clear that she acted as she did not through choice but because of the gods and fate (79, 1639-42).

Menelaus in this play was criticized by Aristotle for being 'unnecessarily bad',[18] but is he really bad, or just weak? He is, admittedly, useless when it comes to assisting his nephew – assistance which Orestes believes he is under a heavy obligation to lend, not just for reasons of family loyalty but also in repayment of an earlier debt owed to Orestes' father Agamemnon (who, it will be remembered, fought a long war in order to get Menelaus' wife Helen back from the Trojans). However, it can seem that Menelaus is motivated more by indecision or cowardice than by malice. Of particular interest is his speech to Orestes (682-716), explaining – or rather failing to explain – just why it will be impossible to help. He seems extremely flustered and doubtful (perhaps more so after listening to Tyndareus' tirade at 607-29), and repeatedly claims that he is

3. Humans and Gods

deficient in strength and resources: he *would* help, if only he could. When Menelaus outlines his parting advice for Orestes, he can only spout clichés about 'waiting for the fire to blow itself out' and 'weathering the storm' (698-701, 706-9).

Nevertheless, it has been pointed out that Menelaus repeatedly evaluates his own and other people's behaviour in terms of 'intelligence' (415, 417, 488, 490, 695, 716) – a habit which, perhaps, marks him out as calculating and devious rather than merely spineless.[19] And, after all, if Orestes were to end up dead or banished from Argos, Menelaus himself might be seen as an obvious candidate to inherit the throne. But it has to be admitted that Menelaus' ruling ambitions are not seen explicitly in the play, even if members of the audience might have been tempted to speculate along these lines. Indeed, the political situation in Argos is so unstable that neither Menelaus nor anyone else could have expected to take over as ruler without a great deal of trouble.

Tyndareus' main function in the play is to oppose Orestes. Predictably, he is furious at his grandson for having killed Clytemnestra: he calls Orestes a 'matricidal serpent' (479 – a description which recalls the imagery of Aeschylus' *Oresteia*), and he says that Orestes has behaved more stupidly than anyone else alive (493). He, like Menelaus, is clearly concerned with 'intelligence' (however we might interpret that quality), and he even refers to his argument with Menelaus as an 'intelligence contest' (491).[20] Tyndareus cannot approve of his daughter's own actions, and indeed declares that he hates impure women (518), but at the same time he believes that Orestes should have behaved in accordance with the *law* (a belief which is stressed by repetition: 495, 500, 503, 523; cf. 512).[21] Tyndareus is certainly an implacable opponent, but critics argue about how reasonable or unreasonable he is. The fact that he goes out of his way to ensure that Orestes dies by public stoning, using his influence to control the Argive assembly (915), may well reveal an immoderately vindictive streak.[22]

The remaining minor characters need not detain us very long. **Hermione**, daughter of Helen and Menelaus, is a young

Euripides: Orestes

woman whose sole purpose is to be kidnapped and used as 'bait' in the final scene. Again, it is hard to uphold the ancient commentator's charge of 'rottenness' when we contemplate Hermione: her role gives her little scope for evil, to be sure, but what strikes us far more powerfully is her youthful innocence, a touching quality which makes her violation seem even more of an outrage. The **messenger** (852-956) merely has to report the off-stage debate in the Argive assembly, in a conventional tragic messenger-speech which reveals little of the messenger's character except his loyalty to the Argive royal family. He provides a striking contrast, however, with the other 'messenger' – the singing **Phrygian slave**, whose elaborate, foreign-sounding aria (1369-1503) is discussed elsewhere. This barbarian is so extravagantly *outré* in his language and mannerisms that his function has sometimes been seen as providing 'comic relief' of a sort (Verrall compared him to the 'Comic Porter' in *Macbeth*).[23] Nevertheless, the sudden change in tone here could also be compared to another scene which is far from 'comic' – the unusual, agonized musical outburst of Aeschylus' Cassandra, just before her death (in *Agamemnon*) – and the distinctively Homeric content of the slave's aria seems to raise more serious issues, including the significance of the Trojan War, the nature of heroism, and (once again) the importance of Helen in past events. The Phrygian may be an extraordinary character, but he is not simply comical or ridiculous.

Finally, the **Argive women**, like other tragic choruses, are conventionally bland and ineffectual. They are sympathetic to Orestes and Electra in their plight, and their assistance is important during the later scenes of conspiracy (1258-1368), though in general their songs convey a distinctly pessimistic attitude towards future prospects for the house of Atreus.

Orestes' dilemma

Did Orestes act rightly when he killed Clytemnestra and Aegisthus? This is the central moral question that the myth raises, but it is difficult or even impossible to answer. In this play

3. Humans and Gods

Orestes and the other characters attempt to explain or justify his crimes by recourse to several different (and conflicting) general principles.

Revenge-killings are not generally deemed acceptable in modern Western thought. But to Greeks of the archaic and classical period, revenge, even when it took the extreme form of violence or murder, was not necessarily seen as wrong: it could be justified on social and religious grounds. As Mary Whitlock Blundell has shown, in an excellent study of Greek ethics and tragedy, 'Greek popular thought is pervaded by the assumption that one should help one's friends and harm one's enemies'.[24] (Compare Menelaus' words at 486: 'It is the custom among Greeks always to honour one's own kin.') This assumption could influence private behaviour, but it also determined public laws. Homicide law, at Athens and elsewhere, which demanded the execution of convicted murderers, was essentially based on the principle of reciprocal killing – a life for a life. According to this principle, then, since Clytemnestra and Aegisthus had killed Agamemnon, they themselves deserved to die in return.

However, the rule of 'helping friends and harming enemies' comes unstuck in this case, because the categories of 'friends' and 'enemies' are mixed up. The killers and victims all belong to the same family, so they are simultaneously both 'friends' and 'enemies': thus the principle becomes unworkable. Either to take revenge or *not* to take revenge would be wrong according to the 'help friends/harm enemies' code, but to kill one's own husband or mother is also wrong according to religious principles and ordinary human decency. Comparatively little is made here of the murder of Aegisthus, who (as the usurper of Agamemnon's throne and the illicit lover of Clytemnestra) was clearly an enemy of Orestes; but Aegisthus was also (as the son of Thyestes and uncle of Orestes) a member of the family, so even his murder is problematic.

Nevertheless, it is made clear that Orestes acted not simply in accordance with this reciprocal principle, nor even out of free will, but because he was prompted to do so by Apollo. As Electra says, despite the fact that some people would deem Orestes'

Euripides: Orestes

behaviour infamous, it is hard to accuse a god of injustice (28-31). Repeatedly it is stressed that Apollo is more to blame than Orestes (75, 161, 191, 275, 417, etc.). If a god is really to blame, it seems unjust that Orestes should now be suffering divine punishment. This is one of the major problems of the play, which the characters and chorus repeatedly try to explain (161-5, 191-3, 316-50, etc.) – why is it that Apollo would induce Orestes to do something that would lead to such horrendous consequences? Indeed, Orestes is so bewildered by his ordeal that he imagines that Agamemnon himself, if he could speak from beyond the grave, would have begged him not to kill Clytemnestra on his account (288-93).

One explanation for Apollo's involvement goes back much further in time: inherited guilt is another causal factor at work behind the play's events. In the prologue and elsewhere (4-27, 807-30), the sufferings of the family are traced back to Orestes' great-grandfather Tantalus, whose 'unchecked tongue' – he revealed the gods' secrets to humans – led to his eternal punishment. His crime led to a hereditary curse on the house. Tantalus' son Pelops tricked Oenomaus' charioteer Myrtilus into sabotaging his master's chariot, in order that he might marry Oenomaus' daughter Hippodamia: Oenomaus was killed, but Pelops also murdered Myrtilus, thus meriting an additional curse. His 'fatal chariot-ride' and its consequences are repeatedly referred to by the chorus (971-1012, 1537-48). Next in line were Pelops' sons Atreus and Thyestes, whose quarrel resulted in Thyestes' unknowingly eating his own children, served up to him by Atreus (15). Atreus' sons both suffered disasters: Menelaus had to fight a war because of his unfaithful wife, and Agamemnon had to sacrifice his daughter Iphigenia in order for the Greek fleet to sail. It was in return for this – perhaps – that Clytemnestra killed Agamemnon, though (as Electra pointedly reminds us, 26-7) her motives were actually rather obscure.

Viewed in the light of heredity, Orestes' conduct is easier to understand (if not forgive). Curiously, though, when Orestes comes to defend himself in the debate with Tyndareus (544-604), he makes comparatively little mention either of the gods

3. Humans and Gods

or of past crimes in the family. He invokes Apollo at the end of the speech (590), but his self-justification and Tyndareus' criticism are based mainly on general principles. Orestes begins and ends by asking: 'What *ought* I to have done?' (551, 596), emphasizing the impossibility of his position in either taking or not taking revenge on his father's behalf. He goes on to explain why he took his father's rather than his mother's side, drawing attention to her *affaire* with Aegisthus (558-63): Iphigenia's death is not mentioned, and Clytemnestra's motives are explained purely in terms of sex. Orestes next makes the surprising declaration that he is a benefactor to all mankind, since his killing of Clytemnestra will have acted as a deterrent to any other wives planning to murder their husbands. This is a peculiar argument, as it requires us to see husband-murdering as a 'general custom' in Greece (*nomos*, 571); Odysseus' wife Penelope is cited as a counterexample to such behaviour (588).

Orestes refers back to the principle of reciprocity later on, when he is trying to persuade Menelaus to help him. But his application of the principle to his present situation is somewhat disturbing. 'I am a criminal,' he says, 'and *to balance this evil* I need to get a crime from you, just as my father Agamemnon criminally assembled the Greek army and went to Troy [...] to put right the folly and misdeeds of your wife' (645-50). He proceeds to 'bargain' with what he sees as their respective obligations: 'As for the slaughter of my sister at Aulis, I will allow you to have that – you do not have to kill Hermione' (658-9). This argument almost reduces the principle to absurdity, because Orestes seems to think that it would be possible to draw up an 'account-sheet' of human behaviour:

debit	**credit**
murder of Agamemnon	murder of Clytemnestra
murder of Iphigenia	[murder of Hermione]
Agamemnon helps Menelaus	Menelaus helps Orestes

His calculating attitude has made many readers feel rather queasy. Can the books really be balanced in this way? Are we

Euripides: Orestes

to question the moral principle itself, or is it just Orestes' own interpretation of the principle that is wrong? As ever, there is no simple answer to these questions. We can choose to see Orestes as cynical or amoral, or we can see his words here, perhaps, as a sign of his increasing desperation.

If a solution to these problems is to be found at all, it will have to involve breaking the rules somehow. In Aeschylus' *Oresteia*, the solution was found in the form of Athenian political institutions – specifically, in the trial presided over by Athena and the establishment of Areopagus as a lawcourt.[25] But in *Orestes* no such solution is forthcoming. On the contrary, Euripides has replaced the famous trial at the Areopagus with a meeting of the Argive assembly – a scene which recontextualizes and updates the Aeschylean version of the myth, but which (more importantly) problematizes Athenian politics and the idea of justice in general.[26] As we shall see (below), the eventual outcome of the assembly, as engineered by Apollo, is very different from the end of the *Oresteia*. Orestes obtains purification, and the cycle of revenge and violence in the household comes to an end, but this time there are no very clear implications for justice or morality. The fact that the gods are still presiding over all this human mess, as ever, is unlikely to make us feel any better about it.

The gods behind the scenes

The central god is Apollo, who seems to have been somewhat of a preoccupation of Euripides in old age: the god and his prophecies are at the heart of several late works, including *Ion* and *Iphigenia among the Taurians* as well as *Orestes*. But the characters and chorus throughout the play make several references to other deities and supernatural forces whom they see, rightly or wrongly, as being at work behind the scenes. As in all tragedies, the human characters do not really understand what is going on. Even when, as here, they hear the final words of a *deus ex machina*, these words only provide a partial explanation. Meanwhile, in their efforts to comprehend what is happen-

3. Humans and Gods

ing to them and why they are suffering so much, the characters invoke a miscellaneous range of supernatural powers. If we try to reconcile their various views into a coherent theological outlook, or if we try to extract from them (as scholars used to do) Euripides' own theological beliefs, we will quickly hit a dead end. The point is that the characters' views are a hopeless mish-mash of conflicting beliefs: they are trying, but failing, to interpret their lives in a broader context.

Orestes' conversation with Menelaus (416-20, 423-4) provides one illustration of this desperate incomprehension:

> *Orestes*: It was Apollo who ordered me to carry out the murder of my mother.
> *Menelaus*: In that case, Apollo is rather unintelligent as regards right and just behaviour.
> *Orestes*: We are slaves to the gods – whatever gods are.
> *Menelaus*: Well, then – does Apollo not relieve you in your ills?
> *Orestes*: He is waiting: that is only natural for a god.
> [...]
> *Menelaus*: How quickly the Furies have come after you because of your mother's blood!
> *Orestes*: The god may not be intelligent, but he is true to his friends.

These lines are striking because of their repeated mention of 'intelligence', the quality which (as we have seen) is somewhat suspect. Both Orestes and Menelaus claim that the god lacks intelligence – but how would they know? Similarly, Orestes' assertion that gods tend to 'wait' before helping humans does not sound too confident: it is really another sign of his own lack of knowledge regarding Apollo's behaviour in the future.

Passages like this can be hard to interpret: what sort of attitude to the gods is being expressed? In older scholarship one often encounters the view that Euripides was an 'atheist'. This view – like many views about Euripides that still persist in some form or another – is partly derived from the inaccurate

Euripides: Orestes

ancient biographies of the poet: the *Lives* record that Euripides was noted for his unorthodox theological views. In turn, the biographers were probably relying on the 'evidence' of comedy: Aristophanes often seems to have cracked jokes about the tragedian's supposed 'atheism' or impiety.[27] But, leaving aside the unanswerable question of what Euripides 'really' believed, his plays do not contain views which can be described as atheistic (a label which would be anachronistic, since it really reflects a Judaeo-Christian type of outlook).[28]

The plays always take the gods for granted – but that does not mean that they never express a sceptical or critical attitude towards them. It may be more helpful to regard Euripidean (and other) tragedy as questioning and exploratory in outlook – a spirit that well reflects the intellectual climate of its time and the nature of Greek religion in general.[29] For the Greeks, to believe in and worship their gods did not mean that they expected to *understand* the gods; and they certainly did not expect that the gods would always treat them with love or kindness. Worshipping the gods in fifth-century Greece (or, for that matter, mythical Argos) certainly did not imply the unquestioning acceptance of any particular set of beliefs or doctrines, nor did it preclude criticism of the divine powers.

Orestes' phrase 'whatever gods are' (418), like similar phrases in Euripidean tragedy, has sometimes been seen as an expression of disbelief,[30] but it can be interpreted more literally in its context as hopeless ignorance leading to frustration. Orestes does not really doubt that the gods exist, but he does not understand why they treat him as they do; and, in particular, he is confused and disappointed by Apollo's treatment of him.

The relationship between Orestes and Apollo can be seen as absolutely central to the play (as well as being typical of the ancient Greek conception of divine power). Although Orestes' terrible acts are explored in the light of other factors (such as the political situation in Argos, the nature of the other characters involved, and the problem of heredity), and although the issue of reciprocal revenge can be treated in terms of a principle

3. Humans and Gods

in (purely) human ethics, it is the divine aspect of Orestes' revenge that really stands out, in this play and in the mythical tradition as a whole. The crucial fact, however we interpret it, is that it was specifically Apollo who required Orestes to murder his mother. The situation requires that Orestes should become, essentially, Apollo's agent, and yet, frustratingly, his relationship with the god seems to be no closer or more privileged for that. Despite fulfilling the role of agent, against his own will and in the face of overwhelming pressure to act otherwise, Orestes is compelled to endure awful suffering and agony. Nor is he granted any special insight into the god's behaviour or the workings of the universe as a whole. Orestes may hope that the god is his 'friend' (424), but for most of the play's length it is really his human 'friends' who seem to be important to him.

Apollo may be the most significant god in *Orestes*, whose name is more frequently mentioned than any other, but he is not the only god at work in the play. Also of great importance are the Erinyes (Furies), though it is never entirely clear how their powers operate, or what the precise relationship is between these gods and other forces, such as Apollo, Zeus or fate (37-8, 163-5, etc.). Sometimes it seems that the Erinyes are deities pursuing private vendettas on behalf of individuals (288-93, 582);[31] at other times it seems that they are independent goddesses of revenge (37-8, 834); while it can also seem that they are controlled directly by Apollo (255-60, 1648-52). At the end of the play it transpires that all these gods are more or less working in unison, under the overall control of Zeus (1684-8), but for most of the play's duration this remains obscure. Indeed, Orestes confesses that he was unsure whether the voice he heard was that of Apollo or some other, anonymous vengeance-demon (*alastôr*, 1668-9), and the chorus, similarly, wonder from time to time whether an unknown *alastôr* is really responsible for the chaos in Argos (337, 1546). At one point, curiously, Electra even tries to persuade Orestes that the Erinyes are only figments of his imagination (259).

In many places the characters refer, vaguely, to unnamed 'gods', plural or singular (2, 19, 418, 579-84, 685, 708-9, 974, etc.) or *daimones* (342, 667), or more impersonal powers, such as 'fate' (*moira* or *moron*, 374, 978, etc.), 'chance' (*tychê*, 635, 716, 1241-5, etc.), 'necessity' (*anankê*, 715, 1012, etc.), or 'the powers that be' (*to theion*, 266-7, 420). These various supernatural powers are sometimes described as if they were interrelated in some (not very clear) way, and sometimes as if they operated independently of one another. No clear pattern emerges from any of this speculation. But at the end of the play, in any case, Apollo makes no mention of any other powers except the Olympian gods. This surely means that the characters were wrong – if Apollo's words are true.

It is interesting to note that the humans also invoke a number of personified abstractions, whom they treat as if they were gods. Electra in her first monody prays to 'Mistress Night', who is imagined as coming up from the Underworld (174; cf. Orestes' words at 1225). The chorus later sing of personified Justice (1242) and Strife (1002-4): this latter divinity is depicted in fully anthropomorphic form, riding on the horses of the goddess Dawn.[32] Most interestingly of all, Orestes, on wakening, prays to 'Mistress Oblivion', whom he praises thus: 'How intelligent you are, and how worthwhile it is for those who suffer misfortune to pray to you!' (213-14). This invocation is highly significant because it implies that Oblivion may have more power than Apollo and the other gods; and when Orestes calls Oblivion 'intelligent', he uses precisely the epithet which he later denies to Apollo (416-24, quoted above).

It is unclear to what extent these abstractions would have been envisaged as real gods. Clearly the characters are praying to them, and it is hard to read such prayers simply as figures of speech, given the Greeks' attitude to 'ill-omened' language. At the same time, these are not gods to whom ritual could be offered. It is difficult to relate these abstract 'gods' to Greek religious views in general,[33] but perhaps the characters' invocations of these strange powers would have been taken as a lack of confidence in the traditional gods of ritual – or, alternatively, as a sign that the characters are, more than ever, clutching at straws.

3. Humans and Gods

Apollo's final solution

By line 1624, events have reached crisis point. Orestes' and Menelaus' final negotiations have failed; the kidnappers and their hostage are trapped on the roof; the Argive mob, armed and carrying blazing torches, are about to storm the palace. What way out can there be from this situation?

All of a sudden, and without warning, Apollo appears on the *mêchanê* – the 'god from the machine' in a literal sense – and shouts 'Stop!' (1625). This interruption is surprising enough in itself, but even more startling is the fact that Apollo has Helen by his side: 'Here she is, this woman whom you see in front of you at the gates of heaven, safe and sound, and not in fact done to death by you' (1631-2). Having thus stopped Orestes and Menelaus in their tracks, Apollo proceeds to 'solve' all the characters' problems in a mere thirty-one lines (1635-65). Helen, it now appears, was rescued from death by Apollo and is to be deified: thus Menelaus will have to take another wife (who will she be?) home with him. Orestes will go into exile and stand trial at Athens (thus, finally, linking up the plot of *Orestes* with the 'authorized' version of the myth familiar from the *Oresteia* and elsewhere), but he will be acquitted and return to rule Argos – and then he will marry Hermione! Electra and Pylades will also be joined in marriage. Orestes finally acknowledges the wisdom and power of Apollo and his oracle (1666-72), and the play closes.

But what sort of closure has been achieved? Perhaps some members of the audience would have felt that this neat and tidy ending, in which the main characters all end up married to one another, is 'happy' – or even 'comic'.[34] Of course, *Orestes* is not the only tragedy to have a seemingly happy ending, but the type of 'happiness' here is somewhat more complex than what we find at the end of a play by (say) Oscar Wilde or P.G. Wodehouse. Indeed, it may have left many others in the audience feeling more uncomfortable. One critic has written that the final scene 'is transparently perfunctory and ironical ... of all the like scenes in Euripides it is perhaps the most prodigiously absurd, unreal, meaningless, impossible'.[35]

Euripides: Orestes

Many other readers seem to agree that a real, *satisfying* sense of closure (in emotional or intellectual terms) is being deliberately withheld by Euripides.[36] At any rate, Apollo's intervention, while it does restore the myth to its normal course, does not resolve the central moral dilemma of Orestes, nor does it explain why his family have for so long been troubled by violence and murder. Nor, crucially, does Apollo explain just how he will 'set things right' in Argos so that Orestes can go on ruling (1664): the political problems of the city are just brushed aside. There is no real possibility of 'learning through suffering', as there was for the characters in the *Oresteia*. We have watched the characters in *Orestes* acting fallibly, even terribly, and now the natural outcome of their actions has been arbitrarily altered at the last minute; but in the process neither they themselves nor the audience have learnt anything about justice or morality. As one critic has written, Apollo's superficial solution 'alters nothing of what the play had shown about human helplessness'.[37]

The ending leaves behind all sorts of other unanswered questions and difficulties. For example, if all the main characters really are 'rotten' (as claimed by the *hypothesis*-writer), it may strike us as outrageous or ironical that they are apparently being rewarded with good fortune. Apollo does not justify his dispensation of outcomes: it is simply divine will, and that is meant to be enough. However, to receive confirmation that the gods were responsible for everything that has happened does not satisfy our desire to see justice or morality at work in the world. Of course, as I said above, the Greeks did not always expect their gods to act justly or to care greatly for humans, as is shown particularly in this play by the relationship between Orestes and Apollo. But, even so, the explanation which Apollo gives for the Trojan War seems to show that the gods' attitude to human life is not just uncaring but breathtakingly cruel and capricious: Zeus and the others simply wanted to make the earth a little less heavy than before (1639-42).[38]

Apollo also reveals (1683-90) that Helen, as a goddess, will in future be worshipped, along with her brothers the Dioscuri, and

3. Humans and Gods

that she will forever afterwards be known to sailors as 'mistress of the watery sea' (1689-90). This detail has troubled certain critics, who point out that even though Helen was associated with the Heavenly Twins in ritual, there is no other evidence that she received cult worship (*theoxenia*) along with them. Was there ever such a cult? Perhaps the aetiology is a fabrication (in which case, presumably, its effect would be to undermine our faith in Apollo's final words).[39] But even if one does not believe that Euripides invented aetiologies, it might still seem ironically inappropriate that mariners should pray to Helen, who was responsible for the sinking of so many Greek and Trojan ships.

The play's ending may not be wholly *satisfying*, then, in the sense that there are plenty of loose ends remaining untied. But we do not have to see this lack of closure as somehow a fault in design – far from it.[40] In fact, the absurd finale is a dramatically effective and entirely appropriate way of rounding off this strange, difficult play. Euripides can be seen as deliberately eluding closure, by giving his audience an unsatisfyingly ironical ending that leaves all the big questions unanswered. But what did the spectators feel, as they left the theatre and walked back home? If they (like so many modern readers) preferred difficulty and ambiguity to neatly wrapped-up texts, perhaps they went on their way both challenged and delighted. Perhaps some of them really did find it all rather hilarious. But for a few, at least, *Orestes* will have left behind a curiously bitter taste.

4

Late Euripides

Criticism of the 'biographical' kind, which interprets literature in the light of what is known about its author's life and views, is currently out of fashion. This is not merely the result of recent theoretical trends which downplay the role of the author in the creation of meaning. In the field of classical studies, it is due more to the wretched state of the evidence: we know almost nothing about our authors and their lives. Nevertheless, when we encounter a work of literature, we cannot help wanting to know something about its author and the times in which he lived. Whenever we read a book or watch a play, it is hard to suppress our instinctive feeling that the artist's own personality or view of the world is emerging from it in some sense.

As I explained in Chapter 1, our information about the historical Euripides is very unreliable. But we do know for certain that *Orestes* is a *late* work, written during the last couple of years of Euripides' long life. Quite by accident, it also happens to be one of the latest surviving Greek tragedies. These facts have strongly influenced the critical reception of *Orestes* in various ways. This chapter aims to unpack the notion of 'lateness' and to show how it can be a help as well as a hindrance to the reader.

Euripides in the ancient biographical tradition

The ancient biographies, for all their problems, paint a vivid picture of Euripides which has proved surprisingly influential and enduring. Many have thought that there is something about this Euripides that somehow rings true, despite the

4. Late Euripides

factual inaccuracies. The biographers describe the playwright as a morose, difficult man who grew progressively more isolated and disenchanted with the world as he approached old age. Unpopular with his friends and with the public at large, rejected by his wife, cuckolded by his slave, embittered against women, the Euripides of the *Lives* came to loathe the company of other people. It is reported that he spent a lonely and disillusioned old age in a sea-cave at Salamis, gloomily looking out at the waves, before finally leaving Athens altogether for Macedon, where he met a hideous death (the details of which recall his own *Bacchae* as well as Aristophanes' *Women at the Thesmophoria*).[1] Even if much of this information is really fictional, it still constitutes a form of critical response to the plays. The Euripides of the biographical tradition has been seen as the sort of man who *could* plausibly have written these plays: a maverick figure, at odds with his time, producing startlingly unusual, difficult, pessimistic drama – almost, perhaps, a sort of 'Outsider' figure.[2]

The ancient *Lives*, as well as describing the 'historical' Euripides, also have certain more objective observations to make about his contribution to the development of tragedy. They stress his numerous technical innovations (including his use of rhetoric, his prologue-speeches, his recognition-scenes and other plot devices), his verbal and philosophical sophistication, and his progressive-sounding music and lyrics.[3] These observations about later Euripidean style are also echoed in Aristophanic comedy (*Frogs, Women at the Thesmophoria* and other plays).

These two separate strands in the ancient biographical tradition – Euripides as 'outsider' and Euripides as 'innovator' – are reflected in much of what has subsequently been written about the playwright. Nineteenth- and earlier twentieth-century European scholars, in particular, used this material – for all its faults – to create an enduring image of the art and personality of Euripides in his later years. The most influential writer of this type was Friedrich Nietzsche, whose first major work, *The Birth of Tragedy* (1872), described *inter alia* the

Euripides: Orestes

development of tragedy at the end of the fifth century.[4] According to Nietzsche, at this time the tragic genre was not simply developing but actually being destroyed – in Euripides' hands, it had changed so much from its roots as to be unrecognizable. We are told that Euripides, 'in the evening of his life', subjected tragedy to a suicidal 'death-struggle':

> What didst thou mean, o impious Euripides, in seeking to subdue this dying one to thy service? Under thy ruthless hands it died: and then thou madest use of counterfeit, masked myth, which like the ape of Heracles could trick itself out in the old finery. And as myth died in thy hands, so too did the genius of music ...[5]

Nietzsche's highly poetical and idiosyncratic account of Euripides influenced other scholars in the Germanic tradition, such as Schlegel, Nestle and others, for whom the category of 'late Euripides' came to embody a particularly problematic view of tragedy and its relationship to the world.[6] The image of the elderly poet, disillusioned with life and also with the art of tragedy, pervades modern studies of Euripides. As Walter Krantz typically expressed it, 'we are in the period of a complete transformation in Euripidean tragedy ... A new "Tragic" is taking shape: it is the fruit of a new view of life, one that inclines more towards resignation and despair than towards heroic struggle and resistance.'[7] Karl Reinhardt, in a well-known article entitled 'The Intellectual Crisis in Euripides', argued that *Orestes* in particular represents the 'final stage' for tragedy, and compared Euripidean 'nihilism' to modern European existentialism.[8]

This type of view is not confined to decades-old German scholarship. For example, Slobodan Unkovski, the director of the most recent production of *Orestes* (performed at Epidaurus in August 2008 by the National Theatre of Northern Greece), gave an interview to the Greek newspaper *Kathimerini* in which he outlined his vision of the play. 'When writing what was probably his last play,' Unkovski said, 'Euripides was very

4. Late Euripides

bitter. He maintained the tragedy structure but at the same time, because of his own problems, he attempted to comment on the gods.'[9] Unkovski does not give details of his sources for the 'bitterness' and 'problems' of the elderly poet, but it is interesting to see that the traditional view of late Euripides continues to cast a very large shadow over modern productions.

Recent scholars, too, have taken a very similar approach, mixing together discussion of the poet's life *and* the external form, content and 'message' of his plays, as if these separate considerations were inextricably linked. For instance, Froma Zeitlin describes the author of *Orestes* as a poet 'laboring under intellectual and spiritual discomforts', while the play itself is a 'chaos of forms' which expresses a turbulent and chaotic view of the world.[10] Edith Hall links Euripides' 'ultimate pessimism' to questions of politics and genre, writing that *Orestes* 'not only decomposes and disintegrates the Athenian democratic charter-myth enshrined in the *Oresteia*, but it threatens to dissolve the very genre, tragedy, which had always been the most patent example of Athenian democratic cultural prestige'.[11]

For such interpreters, the supposedly morose personal temperament of the 'historical' Euripides is transformed into a sort of global pessimism which reflects the meaning of the plays themselves. Thus it can appear highly significant that the 'death' of tragedy, and the last years of Euripides' life, coincided with other troubling social and political developments at Athens. Standard histories of the period tend to be marked by a sense of impending crisis and doom – a sense of the end of an era.[12] By 408 BC the 'golden age' of Athenian democracy was over; the most charismatic politicians of the age were dead or banished; the city was rife with political faction, culminating in a series of oligarchic revolutions (from 411 onwards); the Athenians' ambitious expedition to conquer Sicily (414-413) had ended in disaster; their long war with the Peloponnesians (431-404) was as good as lost; the Athenian empire was facing an uncertain future and precarious finances; the city was in the midst of the intellectual crisis of the sophistic movement; and the great literary figures themselves were reaching the end of their careers.

Euripides: Orestes

It would be wrong to deny that there is some truth in this version of events. One cannot read works from the period – for instance, Aristophanes' *Frogs* (written in 405) or the closing books of Thucydides' unfinished *History of the Peloponnesian War* (which breaks off in 409 but was obviously written in the aftermath of Athens' defeat) – without being struck by a certain sense of *fin-de-siècle* doubt and disillusionment. The political uncertainties of 411-410 do seem to have left their mark on *Orestes* (as I shall show in the next chapter). But, on the other hand, it is easy to let our views be unduly patterned and to over-emphasize the supposed finality of these years. The fact that 'the fifth century' was nearing its end is meaningless, since Euripides and his audience did not count in years 'BC'. Athens did lose the Peloponnesian War in 404, but the world did not come to an end, and Athens continued to flourish afterwards. The Athenian democracy was not fatally undermined by the uprisings of 411-404.

Orestes was not literally the 'final stage' for tragedy: Euripides himself went on to write at least three more plays. Nor did tragedy 'die' with Euripides. It can sometimes appear as if it did, since (owing to sheer bad luck) no tragedy later than his *Bacchae* and *Iphigenia at Aulis* survives.[13] But the genre continued to develop, and new writers continued to emerge, for many years afterwards. Admittedly, Aristotle in the *Poetics* does not help matters by writing gloomily of the inferior quality of tragedy in his own day (the mid-fourth century); but the production records and fragments show that the genre was in a healthy state, while archaeological remains from all over the Mediterranean world show that Athenian tragedy continued to be produced in huge quantities, was immensely popular, and was exported further afield than ever before.[14]

There are numerous problems inherent in the 'Nietzschean' view of late Euripides which has dominated scholarship, based as this view is on overly neat general trends and the questionable application of pseudo-biographical data. Athens' crisis was not terminal; tragedy was not really in its death-throes; Euripides may not actually have been an embittered recluse;

4. Late Euripides

questions of form, content and meaning are in fact separable from one another. But, in any case, preconceptions about Euripides' life and career in general can lead us to overlook specific features of individual plays. Euripides' later plays are not at all homogeneous in character, nor do they conform to a supposed pattern of progressive 'destruction' of the genre, in which each play is progressively more experimental in form and more pessimistic in content than the previous one.

Some of the late works – I am thinking mainly of *Helen* and *Iphigenia among the Taurians*, produced in or around 412 – do, despite their surface exuberance, strike me as being among the bleakest, most pessimistic plays ever written.[15] But the same cannot really be said of *Ion* or *Phoenician Women*, which seem to adopt a less awful outlook on the world. *Orestes* itself divides opinion more than the other late plays, with some scholars reading it as an anguished *cri de coeur* and about as many more seeing it as jolly light entertainment.[16] *Bacchae*, produced posthumously with *Iphigenia at Aulis* (and so perhaps Euripides' last play of all), is altogether different in tone, even rather old-fashioned in style – and, unlike the other late plays, it has always invariably been accepted as a 'proper' tragedy. The plays (like *tragôidia* in general) simply refuse to conform to any neat pattern.

Late style

The biographical approach, as traditionally applied to Euripides, has certain limitations. Nevertheless, it may still be helpful to think of *Orestes* as a 'late' play, in a slightly different sense. We have to face the fact that we do not really know very much, if anything, about Euripides' personal circumstances, and it is even more perilous to start talking about his thoughts, intentions or beliefs. Nor do we need to resort to external circumstances or general ideas of decline (in terms of the prevailing political situation, or the state of the art-form itself). All the same, though, Euripides' life – or, more specifically, his age at the time of writing – may be relevant. For we know without

Euripides: Orestes

a doubt that when he wrote *Orestes* Euripides was an elderly poet, coming to the end of his life: he was in his eighth decade (though his precise age is disputed).[17]

The concept of 'late style' may help us account for *Orestes'* distinctive qualities. This term is used by several critics, including Edward Said, whose book *On Late Style* was, ironically, his own final work, published posthumously in 2006. Said argues, persuasively, that 'lateness' is a characteristic feature exhibited by the works of very many great artists in old age. He examines 'late' works from a wide variety of cultures, genres and periods – including Beethoven, Strauss, Shakespeare, Thomas Mann, Jean Genet and others – to show that, despite their differences, they share certain traits.

The most important of the qualities identified by Said is a deliberate difficulty or impenetrable complexity in place of resolution: 'where one would expect serenity and maturity, one instead finds a bristling, difficult, and unyielding ... challenge.' Many late works can seem experimental in mood, and they may also exhibit an apparent disregard for continuity and structure, or what can seem to be 'a careless and repetitive character' in their construction.[18] (These phrases might serve very well as a description of the content and structure of *Orestes,* which so many critics have found variously problematic.) Said also discusses what he calls 'an increasing sense of apartness, exile and anachronism' in the work of many elderly artists: they produce music or literature which somehow goes against the grain.

In a sense, perhaps, this is not so very far from the familiar image of Euripides in his cave, but Said's approach is different (and more satisfactory) in that he sees this 'apartness' as a general characteristic of the artistic temperament at a certain stage of the creative process, rather than as a specific quirk of the so-called 'destroyer' of tragedy. To interpret *Orestes* in the context of 'late style', then, may not lead to a radical re-evaluation, but it may at least persuade us not to view Euripides as an unusually pessimistic poet or as a problematic or maverick figure in relation to the tragic genre.

4. Late Euripides

Orestes as a sequel

Another significant feature of 'late' works for Said, and one which again seems to be highly relevant to *Orestes*, is their 'strangely recapitulatory and even backward-looking' quality.[19] Elderly artists move backwards as well as forwards: they often seem to be revisiting the themes and subject-matter of their own, and other artists', earlier work. This consideration brings us to another sense in which *Orestes* is a self-consciously 'late' play. That is, it invites us to read it as a *sequel*, of a sort, to earlier works.

Of course, most tragedies can be seen as 'sequels' in a broad sense, because they are always designed to be read in the light of earlier works, or, more generally, in the light of the mythical tradition as a whole. Apart from occasional historical dramas such as Aeschylus' *Persians*, or one-off fictional experiments such as Agathon's *Antheus* or *Anthos*, tragedies always stuck to the same mythical subject matter which had been treated many times before by dramatists, lyric poets and rhapsodes. While dramatists might invent material to 'fill in the gaps' (as in the case of *Orestes*, where much of the material is seemingly invented by Euripides), they almost never *altered* the details of the myths as such.

So any tragedy called *Orestes* or *Electra* would inevitably follow a fairly predictable plot: it would naturally be a continuation of an earlier section of a pre-existing narrative (the segment of the myth which deals with Clytemnestra's murder of Agamemnon). In the same way, any tragedy called *Agamemnon* would inevitably continue the story from an earlier point in the myth (such as the sacrifice of Iphigenia, or the feast of Thyestes). But as well as following the myth in general, dramatists would always have been conscious of specific treatments of the same myths by other playwrights, and would therefore have striven to react against, or 'improve' on, these earlier works – a process that has been called 'the anxiety of influence'.[20]

It may seem that the most obvious model (or 'target') for Euripides was Aeschylus' *Oresteia*, which appears to have

Euripides: Orestes

gained 'classic' status remarkably quickly, and which was probably revived in Athens in or around the 420s.[21] In his *Electra*, a few years before *Orestes* (if the conventional dating is correct), Euripides had already produced what looks like a polemical response to the *Oresteia*, especially in the notorious recognition-scene (*Electra* 518-44). As others have pointed out, it may be significant that *Orestes* was produced precisely fifty years after Aeschylus' trilogy – as it might be a deliberate act of homage, or an iconoclastic updating of that famous work?

Nevertheless, as various ancient and modern scholars have shown, Aeschylus is only one among a number of models for *Orestes*. The play is packed full of intertextual allusions which go far beyond references to the *Oresteia* – and, indeed, far beyond versions of the Orestes story alone.[22] For instance (to take a few examples at random): the opening scene in which Orestes sleeps off an attack of madness recalls, by inversion, the opening of *Eumenides*, where it is the Furies who sleep; the sickness and delirium of Orestes is reminiscent of Sophocles' *Philoctetes*;[23] Electra's arch presentation of Clytemnestra's motives (26-7) is probably meant to recall the ambivalence or contradiction inherent in the Aeschylean and Pindaric versions; the bow of Apollo, which Orestes imagines he is using to defend himself against the Furies (268-71), is taken from Stesichorus' *Oresteia*, as is Tyndareus' description of Orestes as a monster at 479-80; the scene where Pylades supports his friend Orestes (790-5) may be modelled on the scene in *Heracles* (1394ff.) in which Theseus supports the sick Heracles; the prayer for help which Agamemnon's children make to his ghost (1225ff.) echoes both Aeschylus' *Libation-Bearers* (479ff.) and Euripides' own *Electra* (677ff.); the murder plot against Helen is reminiscent of the murder plot against Clytemnestra, by the same conspirators, in *Libation-Bearers*;[24] the scene where Helen is apparently killed and the chorus hover expectantly outside the palace (1286-1310) is based on a similar scene in Sophocles' *Electra* (1398ff.) ... and so on. (The commentators supply many more examples of large- and small-scale allusions.) *Orestes* is designed to be watched or read by an audience familiar not just

4. Late Euripides

with Aeschylus but also with Homer, the Epic Cycle, Stesichorus, Pindar, Sophocles and Euripides' own earlier work.

Froma Zeitlin's stimulating article 'The Closet of Masks' is the most detailed study of the play's intertextuality: she traces all sorts of allusions and echoes from a large number of other works, including (unexpectedly) Euripides' *Medea* and Homer's *Odyssey*. For Zeitlin, *Orestes* is not just a 'sequel' but a 'palimpsest' – a text which is almost postmodern in its multiple layers of literary reference (Zeitlin even goes so far as to compare Euripides explicitly to Jorge Luis Borges).[25] Perhaps it is possible to overemphasize Euripides' modernity, but it is certainly true that *Orestes* is unusually literary and allusive: it clearly goes out of its way to position itself self-consciously as the latest work in a long tradition.

One of the oddest features of *Orestes* is that it functions as a 'sequel' to one tragedy in particular: Euripides' own *Helen*.[26] This is rather surprising. A play calling itself *Orestes* raises certain expectations about its likely content: it would be natural to expect a plot much the same as that of *Libation-Bearers* or the two *Electra* plays, in which Orestes carries out the murder of his mother and Aegisthus. That Helen, Menelaus and Hermione should appear on the scene, and play such a prominent part in events, is extremely unexpected: as I said earlier, it is almost as if they have come in by mistake from the wrong tragedy.

This explanation clearly fits in with the play's overall mood of incongruity, which (as I have argued) is a persistent and recurrent feature. But there is another reason apart from incongruity why Euripides might have wanted to revisit *Helen*: it is because he wanted to use *Orestes* to re-examine some of the same mythical and intellectual themes that he had explored in the earlier play. As well as the problems of Agamemnon's children and the Argive royal household, Euripides is making us think about another branch of the doomed family, not to mention the suffering caused by the Trojan War – a frequent preoccupation of 'late' Euripides, seen also in his 'Trojan trilogy' of 415, the two *Iphigenia* plays and others. In addition, *Helen*

Euripides: Orestes

was famous for raising certain philosophical problems about the relationship between reality, illusion and delusion: these problems seem to arise again in relation to *Orestes*.[27] (I discuss the play's philosophical aspects further in Chapter 6 below.)

Many of the audience members in 408 would have recalled *Helen*, not just because it was a recent production (412) but because its plot was so strange. Its action is set not in Sparta or Troy but in Egypt, and Helen herself is presented in a radically new light, emerging as a good and faithful wife – a far cry from the guilty, lust-crazed adulterer of myth. *Orestes*, which follows the more usual myth, makes no explicit reference to the events of *Helen*, and thus is not a 'sequel' in any straightforward sense. Nevertheless, at a number of points it seems to gesture self-consciously toward the earlier play: it does not continue the odd story of *Helen*, but instead it invites the audience to compare and contrast the portrayal of Helen in both versions.

The relationship between the two plays is emphasized very early on in *Orestes*. The very appearance of Helen may already have started us thinking along these lines, but at the end of the prologue Electra makes the connection explicit. Helen has left the stage, to take clippings of her hair as a grave-offering for Clytemnestra, and Electra turns to the audience and cries (126-31):

> O nature, what a great evil you are to mankind! [...] Did you see how she has preserved her beauty by cutting her hair only at the ends? Yes, she is *the same old Helen*. May the gods hate you for having destroyed me, and Orestes, and the whole of Greece!

This is unmistakably a reference to the Helen of four years ago, who did in fact cut off all her hair (*Helen* 1186-9). The self-consciousness of the reference is underlined not only by Electra's direct mode of audience address, but also by the phrase 'same old Helen'. Yet another layer of meaning is added to this phrase by the fact that Aristophanes, in his parody of *Helen* a year after its performance (in the play *Women at the Thesmophoria* of

4. Late Euripides

411), had referred to Euripides' *'new* Helen' – an expression which seems to have become a slogan or catch-phrase, reflecting the notoriety of *Helen* and the unexpectedly altered character of its heroine.[28]

As I said in Chapter 1, Euripides seems to be playing with the fact that different, inconsistent versions of the myth existed. Which Helen is the real one – the new one or the old one? We are bound to approach this question differently if we interpret *Orestes* with *Helen* in mind, especially since one of the main themes of the earlier play was the unreliable nature of myth and the difficulty of ascertaining the truth-value of what we see in front of our own eyes. Whether we see Helen as good or bad makes a big difference – not just in an abstract or intellectual sense, but in a way that reflects directly on the central plot events of *Orestes*. The murder-plot against Helen has often struck readers as unnecessarily vicious, unmotivated or morally reprehensible,[29] but the plotters justify their actions with reference to Helen's 'evil' nature and the suffering she has caused (247-50, 1132-9, etc.). However, if Helen is seen as blameless or (at any rate) ambiguous, her murder, and Orestes' behaviour, is bound to seem even more questionable.

Modernity and the 'New Music'

There are various ways, then, in which *Orestes* can be seen as a 'late' work. But of course 'lateness' (whether in general or in Nietzsche's or Said's sense) does not necessarily imply an obsolescent or moribund character. It may also have connotations of modernity. In many ways, indeed, *Orestes* feels like the work of a much younger poet.

So far we have been concentrating mainly on the *content* of the play and ways in which it might be seen as reflecting its elderly poet's outlook. But the *sound* of the play in performance was also extremely important in creating a sense of modernity – and incongruity – because the choral songs and arias were composed in a brashly avant-garde style now commonly referred to as the 'New Music'. Since music constituted such a

Euripides: Orestes

large part of the experience of tragic drama, the whole 'feel' of the performance would have been very different from watching and listening to a play by Aeschylus or Sophocles. In fact, *Orestes* is not unique in this respect. Euripides was already firmly associated with the new sound, traces of which are seen in *Trojan Women* (in which the chorus explicitly point out that they are singing in 'a strange new strain', *Tro.* 511-2) and, especially, in the solo arias of *Hypsipyle, Helen, Andromeda* and other late plays.[30]

This new style of music, which I briefly described in Chapter 2 above, was markedly different from traditional Greek music in a number of ways, including the flexible use of melody and harmony, the addition of new notes to the scale, the clashing mixture of different tonalities and different rhythms, the wider variety of instrumentation, and the use of imitative sound-effects. Euripides was only one among a number of musicians to develop this new style towards the end of the century. Other notable practitioners included Timotheus, Melanippides, Phrynis, Philoxenus and Cinesias (who mostly composed in different genres, including choral *dithyramboi* and *nomoi* for solo singers). However, an anonymous treatise *On Tragedy* names Euripides in particular as an important innovator,[31] saying that he was the first tragedian to use the chromatic genus (characterized by 'soft-sounding' harmony) and the Ionic and the 'relaxed' Lydian modes. We are also told that he also introduced polychordy, that his music used more scales, tonalities and melodic colours than that of his predecessors, and also that he used the *kithara* (a type of lyre) more frequently.

In addition – a particularly important consideration in the choral songs of drama – the way in which words were set to music was changing. The music now came to take precedence over the words, and less attention was paid to the actual meaning of the lyrics.[32] One of the main ways in which this change shows up in our texts is in the loose syntactical structure of sentences, the 'pointless' repetition of words, and the inclusion of inarticulate or untranslatable words expressing extreme emotion. For example (from the Phrygian slave's aria, *Orestes* 1373-92):

4. Late Euripides

Earth, earth! – gone, gone!
Aiai ...
Where can I flee, foreign women, flying up to grey sky or sea,
which bull-headed Oceanus folds in his arms as he circles the earth? [...]
Troy, Troy! Ah, me! [...]
Swan-feathered whelp of Leda,
Dyshelen, dyshelen,[33] a Fury upon the finely-wrought Apollonian towers,
ottotoi!
Ah, dirges, dirges!
Unhappy land of Dardanus! The horsemanship of Ganymede, bed-mate of Zeus!

It is clear even from a translation that this is very garbled stuff – not quite gibberish, but not quite normal Greek either. We do not need to hear the song to be aware that the literal sense has been subordinated to the music (which, presumably, sounded as weird as the words). The overall effect must have been startling.

It is frustrating that we are unable to *listen* to either the old or the new style of music, so as to appreciate the difference fully. Various modern reconstructions, transcriptions and 'authentic' performances of ancient Greek music are available,[34] but the state of our source-material is such that they can only ever be treated as rough approximations. In any case, they often tend to strike the modern ear, attuned to the Western chromatic scale, as alien: any one example of this 'ancient' music is now no more or less strange than any other.

Nevertheless, a number of literary texts from the late fifth century describe both the sound of the New Music and its effect on contemporary audiences. For example, Aristophanes in *Frogs* shows that Euripides was firmly associated with the musical revolution, producing a devastatingly accurate parody of his new-style choral odes and solo arias (*Frogs* 1309-63); he also sends up the dithyrambic style of Cinesias and others

Euripides: Orestes

(*Birds* 903, 1373 etc.). Another comic poet, Pherecrates, in his play *Cheiron*, featured 'Music' as a character, who complains about her treatment at the hands of the New Musicians as a kind of violation or rape, while the sound of their discordant music is described as 'bendy' and 'twisty', like 'perverse ant-hills' or 'cabbages riddled with caterpillars'.[35]

It is hard to imagine the effect on the listeners of this completely new type of sound that had never existed before. It would have been mind-blowingly different – a completely new sound-world. But this was not simply a musical revolution. It can be seen as reflecting huge changes in society in general – the growth of what has been called a 'generation gap' in late fifth-century Athens.[36] We may compare the invention of jazz music in turn-of-the-century New Orleans and Chicago, or the emergence of rock-and-roll in America and Britain in the 1950s: these musical movements also had a marked social and political significance. To listen (or *not* listen) to jazz or rock-and-roll was an important statement of one's social, ethnic, economic or age-group identity – a clash between old and new, between black and white, between 'high' and 'low' culture (and so on). It is clear that the New Music provoked a similar reaction in Athens: apart from the comic poets' reflection of events, it is particularly interesting to observe the ideological opposition to New Music expressed by Plato and others. For example, in the *Republic* (4.424c) Plato wrote: 'one must beware of changing to a new form of music, since this endangers the entire social structure. The forms of music are never disturbed without unsettling the very constitution of the state.'[37]

One of the most famous and characteristic examples of the New Music is *Persians*, Timotheus' kitharodic *nomos* of c. 410 BC. The surviving fragments of this composition reveal a style and voice which is not only weirdly modern but loudly and aggressively announces itself as such (e.g. frr. 796, 798 *PMG*):[38]

I do not sing the old songs. My new ones are much better.
It is a young Zeus who now reigns; Cronos' reign is in the past. Away with the ancient Muse!

4. Late Euripides

> With my young songs I dishonour the Muse of old. But I exclude no one, young or old, from the effect of my hymns – only those out-dated spoilers of music ...

When reading these lines it is hard not to be reminded of more recent songs such as The Who's 'My Generation' ('Hope I die before I get old ...'), or perhaps the in-your-face challenge posed by punk in the 1970s and 1980s. It is worth noting that several features of Euripides' *Orestes* specifically recall Timotheus' poem: in particular, both the form and the content of the Phrygian's aria (its exuberance and heavily non-Greek character) have been linked to *Persians*. An ancient anecdote even records, for what it is worth, a story that Euripides helped Timotheus write the music for *Persians*.[39]

The musical character of *Orestes* is not an aspect which comes through to us very prominently when we read our texts and translations nowadays, but it would have struck the original theatre audience very powerfully indeed. For Euripides to be associated with this revolutionary new style of music at all, and for him to employ a jarringly contemporary sound in the context of plays which dramatized prehistoric myths, would have seemed shockingly radical. It is precisely the juxtaposition of ancient and modern that is so striking.

'Modern-dress' tragedy and 'authenticity'

Finally, and perhaps most strikingly of all, *Orestes* is a modern tragedy in another sense: it seems to be set in a version of current-day Athens (in 408 BC) rather than in ancient Argos. In other words, it is essentially what we might call a 'modern-dress' tragedy. Now of course, as Patricia Easterling has pointed out in a well-known article, *tragôidia* of all periods was in the business of performing a balancing-act between past and present, since one of its purposes (she argues) was to recontextualize the ancient myths, making them relevant to the everyday life and experience of the audience. Thus many tragedies contain deliberately anachronistic details of politics, ritual,

Euripides: Orestes

history, geography, and so on.[40] But *Orestes* is perhaps the most blatantly anachronistic of all.

In our own time, the question of 'authenticity' often arises whenever a new production of a Greek tragedy (or Shakespeare) is unveiled. It can be difficult to know where to stand on this question. Some modern productions do seem egregiously to be pushing the limits of taste and acceptability – one reads of all-female productions of *Oedipus* in Manx, or re-interpretations of *Prometheus Bound*, set against a backdrop of the American moon landings – but all the same it is hard to maintain an attitude of absolute purism. What would a truly 'authentic' production look like? We know far less than we would like about original performance conditions in Athens; and, in any case, a modern attempt at performance in ancient Greek with only three actors would seem pedantically over-formal and stilted. More importantly still, it is hard to decide what period a production should be authentic *to* – is it the time in which the plays were set, or the date at which they were first performed? As Easterling has shown, the very conception of Greek tragedy is essentially *in*authentic, in that the plays always tended to 'update' the traditional myths. When we ask 'when were the plays set?', there is no very straightforward answer. All of this means that so-called 'inauthentic' modern productions, which try to make the ancient plays relevant to their own audience are, arguably, truer to the spirit of the original plays than if they were to aim at rigorous authenticity of style.

Orestes takes this process of 'updating' to extremes. One somehow never feels that its action is taking place in its proper mythical place and time – in prehistoric Argos, in the long-ago period just after the Trojan War. There is in fact nothing characteristically Argive about the play's setting. Instead, Euripides has gone out of his way to create a sense of anachronism and alienation, describing the state of Argos, its people and (in particular) its assembly in terms and language that deliberately recall contemporary Athens. This was seen as long ago as 1905 by the Cambridge scholar A.W. Verrall, in his underrated essay on the play:

4. Late Euripides

> Nothing is antique, not even possibly antique, except the names of the *dramatis personae*, whose minds, conduct, and status are, like the surrounding society, absolutely modern. They may call themselves children of Agamemnon or Menelaus, and speak of the Trojan War as a recent event. But the 'Argos', in which they reside, is a fully developed democracy, with a popular assembly as completely sovereign as that of Athens in the age of Pericles or of Cleon ...[41]

Electra, Orestes and the others are presented in the guise of mythical characters, acting out (or, rather, *living* out) well-known events from myth; but at the same time they seem to be incongruously modern and distinctly *un*mythical, as does the world which they inhabit. These characters talk of democratic politics and political factions; they seem conversant with ideas from contemporary philosophy, science and sophistic rhetoric; they adopt a self-consciously detached tone whenever they talk about myths; from time to time they address the audience (as we have already seen in Chapter 1) almost as commentators on, rather than participants in, the action.

Orestes, then, may be seen as late (but not necessarily decadent or destructive), experimental (but not necessarily untragic), difficult (but not necessarily chaotic or intractably pessimistic), self-conscious and allusive (but not necessarily postmodern), and – above all – extraordinarily *new*. We do not know how Euripides felt or what he was thinking when he wrote the play, and in a sense it does not matter. Nevertheless, it is obvious that he was aiming to challenge and surprise his audience, and to make them think about the myths of Orestes, Electra and Helen in a way which was relevant to their own lives and the late-fifth-century world. It remains to explore in more detail just how *Orestes* reflects contemporary society and politics: this is the subject of my next chapter.

5
Politics

Was Athenian *tragoidia* political? It is worth spending a few introductory pages discussing this topic, not just because it is relevant to *Orestes* but because it has been one of the questions most often posed by classical scholars during the last couple of decades. If we look first of all at the circumstances in which the plays were performed, it is hard to resist the thought that the plays were inherently political in some way.

The Greater Dionysia, at which many of the tragedies were staged (along with comedy, satyr-drama and other types of performance), was a major state-sponsored festival held every spring in Athens. This festival was attended not just by Athenians but by many others from further afield, and it seems clear that it constituted an occasion at which Athens' cultural achievements could be displayed to the world at large. But it is important to note that this was not simply a cultural and artistic event. As its name implies, the Dionysia had its origins in religious ritual; but in the fifth century it became, increasingly, a political occasion, one of the largest and most important events in the civic calendar. The Dionysia was run by the city magistrates and involved a great deal of civic pomp and ceremony.

Before the plays began, the audience in the theatre would have been presented with various types of political display, including the dedication of tribute collected from Athens' allies, processions of war widows and orphans, award ceremonies bestowing civic honours on successful individuals, and so on.[1] The drama itself was subject to a high degree of public scrutiny and control. It was a state official (the eponymous archon) who

5. Politics

was responsible for drawing up the shortlist of competing playwrights, and later on the judges were selected from the tribes, and the adjudication took place, in a manner that closely resembled other types of political procedure.[2] A 'theoric fund' which enabled less well-off Athenians to attend the festival was probably established at an early stage, suggesting that the state believed it was important for citizens to watch the performances. What this says about the *purpose* of tragedy is a moot point, but it is clear that the state took a big interest in drama (however we might interpret that interest), and it is also fairly certain that tragedy was seen as popular entertainment rather than 'high culture' for an élite minority.

But what does it mean to ask whether or not tragedy was political? The answer will depend, in part, on who is asking the question. Broadly speaking, any approach which tries to understand the drama in relation to the society that produced it is 'political'. But if we happen to be politicized thinkers with a specific agenda of our own, it will make a difference. If we set out especially to look for political significance (of some sort) in tragedy – or in anything else, for that matter – then we will probably find it. When we frame the question, we must be careful to distinguish whether we are talking about the variety of possible *interpretations* and the *uses* which critics may choose to make of tragedy, or about the *intended effect* of the plays on their audience. If it is the latter, then we have to think about whose 'intention' (itself a problematic concept) is under the microscope. Are we to imagine the author as trying to put across his own political views, or should we be thinking in terms of the Athenian state exercising some sort of control over the plays' political or ideological content? These are complex issues – and, in many ways, insoluble ones, owing largely to the meagre state of our evidence from classical Athens.

Even if we want to read tragedy 'politically', we will have to decide whether or not to do so with specific reference to fifth-century Athenian politics. Does the political significance of the plays relate exclusively to the concerns of one particular city-state at one precise point in time? Or does tragedy have a wider

Euripides: Orestes

significance, of a type that might be relevant to non-Athenians, or non-Greeks – or even modern readers? Aristotle, in the *Poetics*, made a hugely influential case for seeing tragedy as a *universal* genre, which had a social and political function in so far as it propounded general truths about human behaviour. For this reason Aristotle called dramatic poetry 'more philosophical and more serious' than other genres of writing which are more grounded in specific details (such as history).[3] Notoriously, Aristotle omitted all mention of Athenian politics and performance conditions from his discussion of tragedy: as Edith Hall puts it in a well-known essay on the subject, there is no *polis* in the *Poetics*.[4]

'Universalizing' readings find some support in the fact that Athenian tragedy was performed widely outside Athens: the exportability and popularity of the genre, both in mainland Greece and in Sicily, Italy and elsewhere, is well attested during the fifth century and later.[5] Indeed, Athenian tragedies are still performed and enjoyed all over the world by people of diverse cultures to whom fifth-century Athenian politics are a closed book. But another, more obvious, reason for taking a universal approach is that tragedy contains few direct references to contemporary people and events. Its action almost invariably takes place in the world of myth, far removed in time and space from contemporary Athens. Few tragedies are even set in Athens or based on Athenian myths: Thebes, Troy or (as in *Orestes*) Argos are more common settings, though the plays range far more widely. The ostensibly unpolitical, untopical world of tragedy contrasts starkly with that other Dionysian dramatic genre, comedy, which is frequently set in the current-day city of Athens and habitually makes reference to living politicians and current debates. Comedy, unlike tragedy, is undeniably, ostentatiously 'political' – though that certainly does not mean that scholars agree on how to interpret its political content.[6]

On the other hand, tragedy is not completely devoid of references to contemporary life. I have already pointed out that *Orestes* contains a number of such references; but even if *Or-*

5. Politics

estes is unusual, it is clear that many other tragedies make various deliberately anachronistic allusions to fifth-century religious, civic and political institutions.[7] Some tragedies in particular – for example, Aeschylus' *Eumenides* or Euripides' *Suppliant Women* and *Children of Heracles* – have widely been referred to as 'political plays' for this reason. Other plays contain fewer direct allusions to the real world, but there are numerous ways in which tragic performances may be seen as *indirectly* reflecting current politics.

Modern approaches to tragic politics

Modern scholarship has seen several distinctive and widely differing approaches to these issues of 'tragic politics', and it may be helpful to mention some of the most important recent approaches here. (Inevitably, the brief summaries which follow reduce the various scholars' nuanced views to their bare bones, but I have tried to be as representative as possible.) All these approaches focus on the precise relationship between drama and society and on the effect of tragedy on its audience.

Simon Goldhill, in his well-known article 'The Great Dionysia and Civic Ideology', perhaps represents the nearest thing to a current orthodoxy.[8] He sees tragedy as a profoundly Athenian and (specifically) democratic medium, and argues that it is no accident that its fully developed form coincided with the emergence of radical democracy at Athens. Goldhill makes much of the undoubtedly political, non-dramatic aspects of the Dionysia (mentioned above) when arguing that the function of the festival was essentially to promote civic ideology. This view has found wide acceptance: the main objection to it, perhaps, is that it concentrates mainly on the 'framing' ceremonies rather than the actual content of the plays themselves. Also, as Goldhill himself admits, it is rather hard to pin down what constituted 'civic ideology'.

A comparable approach is represented by 'French school' structuralist critics such as Jean-Pierre Vernant and Pierre Vidal-Naquet, who also make ideology central to their view of the purpose of tragedy.⁹ In their important work *Myth and Tragedy in Ancient Greece* they identify the 'historical moment of tragedy' as the early and middle fifth century, which they view as a time of intellectual and political crisis in Athens. For such critics, tragedy is seen, crucially, as breaking down the structures or systems on which civilised society is based, and its meaning derives from the fact that it *questions* civic ideology, either to affirm or to undermine it. Thus tragedy is the genre through which the Athenians came to terms with the massive social and political changes that took place during the fifth century. Critics influenced by the French-school approach tend to write about tragedy in the interrogative rather than the affirmative mode: 'problematization' and 'ambiguity' tend to be privileged over definite answers.

Another influential British scholar, Richard Seaford, also sees tragedy specifically as an institution of the democratic city-state, but his approach distinctively combines politics with religion.¹⁰ Seaford draws attention to the large number of tragedies which contain aetiological myths, thus linking the world of tragedy closely to the real-life activities of many audience members. What we see in many typical tragic plots, he argues, is old-style ruling families being replaced by *polis* institutions such as rituals, law-courts and so on. Dionysus, the god of the theatre, is central to Seaford's interpretation, but rather than being the god of ambiguity (as he was for Vernant and Vidal-Naquet), Dionysus becomes the god of communal activity, almost a 'democratic' sort of deity; and when the tyrants perish it can be seen as a form of 'Dionysiac self-destruction'.¹¹

All these approaches assume that tragedy was both political and (more or less) didactic in nature. Certain scholars (for instance, Neil Croally and Justina Gregory) have gone even further along these lines, seeing tragedy as a vehicle for imparting explicit political 'lessons' to the audience.¹² But this is far from being uncontroversial. Within antiquity, too, certain critics disagreed about the matter. Aristophanes made one of his characters say that the purpose of tragedy was 'to give good advice and make people better citizens in their communities'

5. Politics

(*Frogs* 1008-10), but this may be an ironical joke. Plato sometimes implies that the job of tragedy is to teach political lessons (e.g. *Protagoras* 312a-25a, *Laws* 2.653a-655b), but in the *Republic*, notoriously, he banned tragedy from his ideal state, on the grounds that it dangerously misleads those who watch it.[13] Similarly, in his earlier dialogue *Gorgias*, Socrates compares tragedy to sophistic rhetoric, implying that it *seems* to have a morally edifying 'message' but is really just interested in gratifying its audience:

> What about that grand and wondrous art, the composition of tragedy? Why is it taken so seriously? Do you suppose that the object of its effort and striving is simply to please the spectators? Or does it also struggle to avoid giving them some message which is delightful and charming but wicked, instead talking and singing about things which are improving, though they may be difficult to hear? Which of these two functions do you attribute to tragedy?
> (*Gorgias* 502b1-8)

This dichotomy between 'entertainment' and 'instruction' is important, but also rather artificial (teaching and giving pleasure are not mutually exclusive alternatives, nor are they the only possible functions of drama).

Nevertheless, Plato's discussion of tragedy's purpose has been influential, and several modern scholars in particular (what we might call the 'Oxford school') have taken a broadly Platonic position in denying any serious political or didactic function to tragedy. For example, Jasper Griffin and Scott Scullion both maintain (against Seaford, Goldhill and others) that politics and ritual, while perhaps more important to some plays than others, are of little interpretative importance in general.[14] Such critics suggest that the plays would have provoked their audience to lamentation, pity, fear and similar responses far more often than celebration or ideological deliberation. This type of reading offers a salutary critique of 'orthodox' views, but it seems to be based on a view of the

Euripides: Orestes

average tragic spectator as an oddly apolitical, disengaged sort of person.

Finally, a distinct swing away from Athenocentrism is demonstrated by both Peter Rhodes and David Carter, who argue that tragedy, while admittedly political, is neither inherently democratic nor specifically Athenian. These scholars draw attention to the fact that during antiquity the genre was widely accessible to non-Athenian audiences, and argue (in different but complementary ways) that tragedy's 'ideology', if any, is Hellenic – or even generic, relating to *all* types of community – rather than Athenian as such.[15]

Generic diversity and the plurality of voices

It seems unlikely that the debate will ever die down (at the time of writing it is still most certainly a 'hot' topic in current scholarship). But it is worth pointing out that phrases such as '*the* political function of tragedy' imply that there is a single, overall purpose behind the genre as a whole, and that if we could only discover this purpose it would provide the key to understanding every tragedy. As I have already suggested (in Chapter 1), I think that it is wrong to view *tragôidia* as a homogeneous art-form: the plays are so diverse that it seems unrealistic to search for consistency of theme or purpose. Apart from any other consideration, our surviving tragedies were written over the course of several decades (from c. 472 to c. 406), during which time internal and external politics saw huge changes: it would be strange if the Athenians' 'ideology' (or that of the plays) had remained static during that long period.

It would also be very strange if playwrights, from time to time, did not engage at all (directly or indirectly) with current events. It is hard to conceive of any literary work designed to be read in a total cultural vacuum. But, at any rate, it is always more fruitful to look at individual plays, one by one. Whether we are talking about politics or some other aspect of tragedy, it is better to consider each play on its own terms, rather than '*the* function of tragedy' as a whole. Some of the plays are, clearly,

5. Politics

more or less political than others, depending on the mood of the playwright and the prevailing political circumstances of the particular moment.

The specific question of whether the tragedians (on their own account or on behalf of the state) ever saw themselves as putting forward a definite political *message* is more difficult to answer – but probably it is the wrong sort of question to ask in the first place. The main problem is that the author's viewpoint is absent from the text: no single, authoritative voice tends to stand out clearly from the others. Indeed, one of the ways in which tragedy has been seen as 'democratic' is precisely in its plurality of different voices:[16] tragedy dramatizes debates but stops short of actually solving them. This tendency is seen most obviously in the *agôn* scenes, which – significantly – never end in a conclusion or definite outcome, but instead leave the audience themselves to carry on the debate in their own minds. The same could be said of the form of tragedy as a whole: we are presented with a wide variety of characters and viewpoints, but we are not given the ultimate 'message' or 'meaning' in so many words. Tragedy is more subtle than that, and its messages more elusive.

Even the most apolitical reader would be hard pressed to deny the overtly political content of *Orestes*. Whatever our view of its purpose, it is an unusually (even uniquely) topical tragedy, which, in spite of its supposedly Argive setting, alludes unmistakably to contemporary Athenian politics. Surprisingly, the discussions summarized above have tended to ignore or skate over *Orestes*: the 'tragic politics' debate has usually revolved instead around such plays as *Bacchae*, *Antigone*, the *Oresteia* and so on.[17] Perhaps this comparative neglect can be attributed to *Orestes*' status as an unpopular, non-canonical tragedy. However, it is probably due more to the fact that these other plays can more readily be made to yield up 'messages' when examined closely.[18] But even if political messages of a sort can be uncovered in some plays (an approach which remains highly problematic), *Orestes* seems almost wilfully to defy interpretation. It is undeniably *political*, but does it have a political *purpose* or a didactic message? Very probably not.

Euripides: Orestes

The sections which follow, then, do not attempt to set out a political *interpretation* as such. Rather, they examine various ways in which the play seems to evoke current affairs by way of suggestive echoes and similarities (I do not put it more strongly than that). Before moving on to allusions and anachronisms specific to 411-408 BC, let us begin by examining an issue of more general political relevance – the war.

Reflections on war

Many of the tragedies we now possess, including nearly all of Euripides' surviving works, were written during a time when the Athenians were almost continually at war with the Spartans and their allies – a period (431-404) which we now refer to as the Peloponnesian War, and which its chronicler Thucydides (*History* 1.1) described as 'the greatest ever disturbance in the history of Greece'. It is perhaps no coincidence that, as this exhausting war dragged on and Athens' position worsened, the dramatists wrote more and more plays on the subject of war.

If one stages a play about (any) war at the same time as a real war is going on in the background, there will be no need to draw any explicit parallels between fiction and reality, nor any need for intrusive authorial comment, 'breaking of the illusion' or similar effects. The audience will naturally make the interpretative connection by themselves. When the tragedians presented such plays as *Andromache, Trojan Women, Helen, Orestes,* the *Iphigenia*-tragedies and others on similar themes, it seems inevitable that the audiences would have viewed the action in the light of the war going on around them. This is equally true of modern productions of Greek tragedy in wartime, which have been used as a form of oblique comment on the current conflict. (One calls to mind Tony Harrison's memorable 2006 adaptation of Euripides' *Hecuba* for the Royal Shakespeare Company, which was an unambiguous protest against the British and American 'war on terror'.[19])

It is interesting to note the uses made of the Trojan War in drama (and other types of writing) during the Peloponnesian

5. Politics

War. Thucydides and Herodotus each took the Trojan War as a starting-point for their own histories of contemporary wars, inviting comparison and contrast;[20] the sophist Gorgias wrote speeches about the role played in the war by such figures as Helen and Palamedes; and even the comic playwrights, who (unlike tragedians) could write openly about current events, turned to the Trojan War in order to explore sensitive political questions from a relatively safe distance.[21] All of these writers focus more or less exclusively on questions of causation, justifiability and the human cost of the war. Why did the war start? What caused it? Was it worth going to war at all? What, if anything, did the war achieve? Such questions are asked with relation to the Trojan War, but they can equally well be asked of all wars. In this sense, then, the Trojan War has a political function as a counterpart or 'foil' to the Peloponnesian War.

Furthermore, it is hard not to see a distinct 'anti-war' sentiment in plays such as *Helen, Trojan Women* and *Orestes*.[22] This is partly because they portray in such depth the suffering and misery that war can bring, but also because they seem to exhibit a deep disillusionment. These plays have often been taken as implying that the Trojan War was a mistake, either because its negative consequences outweighed its positive achievements (if any), or because it was fought by morally questionable men for the sake of a worthless woman, or even because it was fought over a phantom (as in *Helen*). When Apollo appears at the end of *Orestes* and reveals the true cause of the Trojan War, it is so trivial as to seem derisory: the earth was, apparently, too heavy, so Zeus and the other gods decided to lighten it a little by relieving it of surplus population (1639-42). This jaw-droppingly cruel and outrageous explanation of all the death and suffering at Troy is precisely the same as that offered in Euripides' *Helen*.[23] All of this may perhaps lead us to reflect on the Peloponnesian War: for what cause was that fought?

Euripides' wartime tragedies also focus on the issue of heroism. *Orestes*, along with other plays, is set shortly after the war has ended, at a time when the great heroes of Troy are returning to – as they hope – normal civic and domestic life.

Euripides: Orestes

Frequently this process of return and reintegration leads to a crisis, and the 'heroes' find their status and worth thrown into doubt. Agamemnon's murder at the hands of his own wife is perhaps the most extreme example of a heroic homecoming gone wrong, but it is not the only instance of the questioning of heroic values in tragedy. As one scholar has written, *Orestes* 'reduces the heroic ethic to malevolent triviality', largely through its presentation of the hero Menelaus as a dithering coward.[24] One might add that Menelaus, though he is given positive attributes in epic, never emerges very well from any of the tragedies in which he appears. No one has ever fully explained this fact, but it may well be connected with his nationality: as a Spartan, he represents the Athenians' great enemy. However, it should be noted that Euripides does not stress the anti-Spartan aspect nearly as much in *Orestes* as (for example) in the earlier *Andromache*, where Menelaus and Hermione appear in a more pejorative – and politicized – light.[25]

Trojan heroism is evoked at one of the oddest moments in *Orestes*, in a way which seems to diminish the scale and significance of those earlier exploits. This is during the scene in which we unexpectedly encounter a 'Phrygian' (the alternative word for 'Trojan' in epic and tragedy). Electra declares that Menelaus is going to find the present situation in Argos more of an ordeal than the Trojan War. This may prompt us to realize that this kidnap-and-murder plot, in which Menelaus tries to rescue his wife from her abductors, is actually a trivialized replaying of the basic pattern of events at Troy. 'Let Menelaus know that he has encountered real men, not cowardly Phrygians!' shouts Electra (1350-2). But a few lines later (in a quite excellent bit of timing), a 'cowardly Phrygian' does in fact appear, in the most bizarre and unthreatening manner imaginable. 'Was it like this at Troy?' Orestes asks, as he holds his sword to the Phrygian's throat (1518): the irony is piquant.

We may well be reminded of the final scene in *Helen*, where Menelaus, again finding himself in a new and strange setting, kills numerous barbarian slaves, and Helen shouts out encouragement: 'Where is the old glory that you had at Troy? Show it

5. Politics

to these barbarians!' (*Helen* 1602-4). In both these plays, the old 'glory' of Troy is severely eroded, the significance of the conflict is questioned, and it is up to us, again, to make what connections we will between ancient and modern wars. As Fuqua puts it in his study of myth in *Orestes*, Euripides is using such scenes to explore the tension between 'the glories of the heroic past' and the political problems of the present.[26] All of this, of course, provides another explanation (quite apart from 'late' self-referentiality and backward glances at earlier literary works – see Chapter 4 above) for the unusual prominence of Helen as a character in this play. Helen, in a sense, embodies the Trojan War – and matters relating to war are of central importance for understanding *Orestes*.

This observation brings us back to the Peloponnesian War, and to the specific problems facing the Athenians at the time when Euripides came to write *Orestes*. As Thucydides describes it, the turning-point in the long war came in 415-414 BC, when the Athenians sent a fleet to Sicily with the intention of conquering the island. The unexpected and total defeat of the Athenian forces less than two years later was a military and financial disaster and a major blow for Athenian morale.[27]

Athens 411-408 BC

> As long as the war was evenly balanced, the Athenians preserved the democracy. But when, after the disaster in Sicily, the Spartan side was strengthened through its alliance with the Persian king, they were compelled to interfere with the democracy and set up the constitution of the Four Hundred.

So runs the calm, sober account of the Aristotelian *Athenian Constitution*, written probably seven or eight decades after the events it describes (spring 411).[28] But the reality must have been far more turbulent: this 'interference' with the democracy was a major revolution, an oligarchic coup which put an end to decades of direct democracy. This huge change in internal

Euripides: Orestes

affairs reflects how desperate the wartime situation had become by early 411 and what a shattering effect the Sicilian defeat must have had on public confidence.

The constitution of the 'Four Hundred' did not last for more than a few months. It was soon overthrown and replaced by a more moderate oligarchic regime, the so-called constitution of the 'Five Thousand' (*Athenian Constitution* 33.1; Thucydides 8.97-8), but this state of affairs was also short-lived, and the democracy was restored in 410. Nevertheless, the return to democratic rule was extremely precarious, not just because of the ongoing war and the problems it created, but also because of the antagonisms within the state which had been aroused by the two coups and their aftermath. It would not be long before Athens lost the war and further oligarchic revolution took place (the rule of the 'Thirty' in 404).

Orestes was written and performed in the midst of all these upheavals. Even though democracy had, in theory, been restored, there must have been a terrible sense of uncertainty about what would happen next in Athens. A general mood of unease prevailed; there were public prosecutions of those who had been involved in the uprisings of 411; Antiphon and Archeptolemus, two of the main leaders of the oligarchic party, were tried and executed, along with many others.[29] Contemporary sources also reflect a change for the worse in the quality of political debate. The most prominent politicians are almost without exception seen as 'demagogues' – figures who presented themselves as champions of the people but who in fact were self-serving, corrupt opportunists.[30] One of the most prominent public figures in the aftermath of the revolution was the radical democrat Cleophon, whom Aristophanes criticizes as one of the corrupt new 'counterfeit' breed of politicians, a barbarian and a warmonger (*Frogs* 679-85, 1532).

Almost every critic who has written on the play has detected a series of suggestive echoes and allusions to these events. Some have gone even further and seen specific similarities, or even a sort of allegorical significance, in certain details. For example, Edith Hall points out, in particular, similarities be-

5. Politics

tween Orestes' situation in the play and that of the oligarchic Antiphon: both make unsuccessful appeals to Sparta for help; both use rhetoric to attempt to sway the assembly; both are tried and condemned by the *demos*.[31] Another recent critic, Christian Wolff, detects in Talthybius (one of the speakers in the assembly-scene, at 888-97) a distinct similarity to Theramenes, the oligarch whose 'adaptability' under various changes of regime had the effect of saving his own skin, at the cost of his good reputation (Aristophanes, *Frogs* 538-9; cf. *Athenian Constitution* 28.5).[32] James Morwood, following an ancient commentator, interprets a reference to 'unscrupulous leaders' (770-1) as a veiled criticism of Cleophon.[33] Even if Euripides himself did not intend his viewers to make these very specific, literal identifications of characters with real-life personalities, it would have been hard for Athenians watching the play in 408 to avoid noticing the similarities (at least). It would also have been easy – perhaps even natural – for them to see Orestes and his supporters as a quasi-oligarchic faction and the other characters as rivals and antagonists, with the nameless mob in the background all along. The parallels, in general and in detail, between Athens and the revolutionary 'Argos' of the play are so numerous that this interpretation is almost irresistible.

Camaraderie

There is much talk of 'friendship' in the play, notably in the depiction of the relationship between Orestes and Pylades.[34] But (as we saw in Chapter 3) Euripides has made it deliberately difficult for us to evaluate the nature of their camaraderie. In fact, there is a markedly political as well as a personal aspect to this relationship. As Elizabeth Rawson demonstrates (following the lead of A.W. Verrall), Orestes' and Pylades' camaraderie is repeatedly described in language which explicitly recalls the *hetaireiai* – the political 'clubs', formed of young aristocratic men and oligarchic sympathizers, which arose in the last couple of decades of the fifth century and had an alarming effect on civic life.[35] The members of these 'clubs' were active in the

Euripides: Orestes

revolution of 411-410, and after the democracy was restored they continued to cause fear and intimidation in the city. Thucydides' description of such factions is often quoted (*History* 3.82: this account of the revolution at Corcyra is generally interpreted as a series of reflections on civil disturbance more generally):[36]

> What used to be described as a thoughtless act of aggression was now regarded as the courage one would expect to find in a *hetairos* [...] Fanatical enthusiasm was the mark of a real man, and to plot against an enemy behind his back was perfectly legitimate self-defence. [...] These clubs were not formed to enjoy the benefits of the established laws, but to acquire power by overthrowing the existing regime; and the members of these parties felt confidence in each other not because of any fellowship in a religious communion, but because they were partners in crime.

In this context, all seemingly innocent occurrences of words such as *philos* ('friend') or *hetairos* ('colleague') in Euripides may take on an extra level of meaning.

Pylades and Orestes even refer to their friendship explicitly as a *hetaireia* (1072, 1079): this pair of references is striking, since the noun is found only once elsewhere in tragedy.[37] Hall also points out that one of the chief functions of a *hetairos* (attested at Thucydides 8.54) was to assist his comrades in lawsuits – precisely the function which Pylades performs for his friend.[38] But it is not just the relationship of the two young men that is significant. The membership of this *hetaireia* also includes Electra, who plays an equally large part in the criminal plot in the second half of the play. At 1190 Orestes refers for the first time to the 'trio of comrades' (*trissoi philoi*), a description which is echoed a few lines later by Pylades in his prayer to Zeus and Justice (1242-5):

> Grant success to Orestes here, and to me, and to Electra as well – for a single contest awaits this trio of comrades,

5. Politics

and a single outcome: we must live or die all together as one.

Electra too refers to their relationship as 'one single compact' (*hen philon*, 1192). As West observes, this scene and its phraseology mark a turning-point in the plot and in the audience's conception of what is at stake: until now, we have been led to see the characters in pairs (Orestes and Electra as the beleaguered siblings; Orestes and Pylades as the plotters), but now it is clear that we are to see them as a group of three.[39] Another level of meaning is added to these prayers and vows if we see in them an allusion to the oaths of loyalty taken by members of *hetaireiai*, as described by Thucydides (*History* 3.82.6: 'Family relations were a weaker tie than membership of a *hetaireia*, since *hetairoi* were more ready to go to any extreme for any reason whatsoever'). Certainly it is hard to deny such an allusion in Orestes' comments at 804-5:

> What you need to do is get yourselves *hetairoi*, not just relatives. Why, an outsider, if he forms a bond with a person through the way he behaves, is a greater possession than countless blood relatives.

It seems, then, that we are being led to interpret Euripides' 'Argos' anachronistically and Athenocentrically, seeing Orestes, Electra and Pylades together as one among a number of clubs and factions in the city. All the ethical questions raised by the traditional revenge-myth are thus altered. Are these the sort of unscrupulous, amoral people who, in these debased times, would kill their parents because they see their *hetairoi* as more important, rather than because they are following divine orders or ethical obligations? Perhaps so; but far from simplifying matters, the political aspect adds a further layer of complexity. When Pylades prevents Orestes from visiting his mother's tomb, saying: 'No – *she* was your enemy. Now come along ...' (798-9), we can read his words, straightforwardly, as a chilling example of the inhuman attitudes of *hetairoi*. Nevertheless, the dramatic context, and the character of Clytemnestra, make things more difficult to evaluate. Clytemnestra may have been Orestes' mother, but she was not a 'normal' mother in any sense. Politics have not replaced or solved the old moral problems, only made them worse.

It is hard to deny all these references to *hetaireiai*; it is harder to decide just what they mean. Rawson was clear in her view that the relationship of the three plotters is to be seen as unambiguously 'evil,' and others have followed her. This hyperpessimistic reading seems irresistible, perhaps, if we read Euripides in the light of Thucydides (quoted above). But (as Porter points out), despite their similarities, the two writers in fact give quite different views of *hetairoi*; and Thucydides cannot straightforwardly be used as evidence for 'the public mood' at Athens in 408: he is writing from his own highly idiosyncratic perspective.[40] Similarly, Christopher Pelling, in his interesting analysis of the play's 'ideology', is reluctant to see the play as straightforwardly condemnatory. In his view, Euripides' mass audience is being invited to 'explore' and 'understand' the motivation and behaviour of members of oligarchic factions.[41]

The debate in the assembly

The verdict on Orestes and Electra is decided by a popular assembly of the Argive people – not, as in Aeschylus' *Eumenides,* by a lawcourt presided over by the goddess Athena (a scenario which *Orestes* evokes by stark contrast). We are not allowed to see this assembly: it is described in a messenger-speech (866-956). This is because of staging conventions and the three-actor rule, which made it impossible to stage the assembly in a realistic way. But the fact that the debate is reported to us at second hand means that the messenger is able to offer a running commentary on the personalities and motives of the participants. This evaluative commentary is important in shaping our response: it is made clear that what took place was a nightmare scenario. The debate seems to exemplify the worst type of behaviour that can take place in a supposedly democratic assembly.

5. Politics

As has been pointed out, the Argive assembly is described in terms which do not *quite* correspond to the Athenian assembly but are so close as to make an identification virtually inevitable. The gathering is called an 'assembled mass' (*ekklêtos okhlos*, 612), which is nearly the same as the Athenian term *ekklêsia*; we know that this gathering has already passed a measure against Orestes and Electra, phrased in language which recalls official Athenian decrees (46); and when the Argive town-crier asks the crowd 'who wishes to speak?' (885), he uses a formula which paraphrases rather than directly quotes the Athenian equivalent.[42] All these allusions, on top of the general similarity of the situations, show that 'the Argive assembly' is indeed, to all intents and purposes, a version of the Athenian assembly.

Most people have, again, been inclined to read the debate in the light of Thucydides, and his description of what it was like in the Athenian assembly during the oligarchic revolution (*History* 8.66) is frequently quoted:

> The Assembly and the Council chosen by lot continued to hold meetings. However, they took no decisions that were not approved by the party of the revolution; in fact all the speakers came from this party, and what they were going to say had been considered by their party beforehand. People were afraid when they saw their numbers, and now no one ventured to speak in opposition to them. If anyone did venture to do so, some appropriate method was soon found for having him killed ...

There is no specific relationship between the two texts (in terms of the 'influence' of one on the other), but nevertheless Euripides' debate scene reflects a similar general mood and character. Also, like Thucydides, he shows that the 'debate' here is being manipulated by certain unscrupulous individuals and groups who have the outcome virtually sewn up in advance.

When the messenger arrived to take his seat on the hill of Danaus, a large crowd had already assembled, and the scene he encountered was so tense and agitated that he took it to be the

Euripides: Orestes

response to a declaration of war by one of Argos' enemies (871-6). His speech conveys a strong sense of the hubbub, noise and active engagement of the assembled people (the crowd's responses – murmuring, shouting, indications of approval or disapproval – are mentioned at 875-6, 894, 901, 902, 930, 943).

The first speaker, Talthybius, is characterized by disloyalty and 'double talk' (890). We learn that he is prone to change his allegiance to anyone who happens to be in power (889), so that even though he was formerly a supporter of Agamemnon and his family, he is now buttering up the *philoi* ('friends'? 'supporters'? 'club'?) of the murdered Aegisthus (894-5). This rival faction is seen as a powerful, dangerous and highly influential group within the city (896-7). The messenger adds that Talthybius, as a herald, belongs to a recognizably fickle 'type', which tends to pander to those in power: this rather incongruous comment may be an interpolation. It may seem strange that a general point about heralds should be made here, but, alternatively, the lines may contain a specific comment on an individual politician: as mentioned above, some scholars have seen 'Talthybius' here as a thinly disguised version of the oligarchic turncoat Theramenes.

Diomedes, who speaks next, adopts the more moderate (and religiously correct) proposal that Orestes and Electra should be punished by exile. It is significant that this balanced, humane viewpoint is virtually ignored: Diomedes' speech is summarized in just two lines (899-900), and elicits only a muted, ambivalent reaction from the crowd. More space is given to the speaker who follows, an anonymous personage who is awarded an extravagantly pejorative epithet: 'impossible to shut up, fiercely audacious, an Argive not worthy of the name, driven to extremes, reliant on shouting and stupid drivel' (903-5). The transmitted text in fact continues in this vein for some lines (906-13), drawing general conclusions about the harmful effect on the city of such outspoken characters, but nearly all editors delete these lines as a clumsy later addition.[43] This anonymous 'demagogue' advocates the penalty of death by stoning. We are told that he is a mouthpiece for Tyndareus' views (915), which

5. Politics

comes as no surprise following the earlier *agôn*-scene (607-29), but we may still find it disturbing that the Spartan aristocrat Tyndareus can exert such an influence on the Argive rabble-rousers, and this fact may reflect unease about Spartan influence on Athenian politics in 408.

The next speaker is again anonymous, but much more sympathetically portrayed: he is a simple, honest farmer who speaks in support of Orestes and condemns Clytemnestra's behaviour (917-29). His argument is somewhat astonishing, since he claims that Orestes deserves not punishment but reward, in the form of a civic crown (924). West suggests that there may be another oblique contemporary reference here, to the fact that in 409 a civic crown was awarded by the Athenians to the killer of the oligarchic leader Phrynichus. The messenger tells us that, though 'decent people' approved of the farmer's proposal (930), it was not adopted. Nor does the crowd respond favourably to the final speech, a misjudged address delivered by Orestes himself (932-42), in which he claims to have acted as a public benefactor. The vote is taken (by show of hands), and the verdict of the assembly – which never really seemed in doubt – is that the proposal of 'the bad man' should be accepted (944).

The play's image of the Argive (= Athenian) assembly and of political life in general is overwhelmingly negative; but so far we have been concentrating mainly on specific individuals and groups. The final section below takes a closer look at the play's presentation of the *dêmos* as a whole.

The people of Argos/Athens

In her essay 'The Sociology of Athenian Tragedy', Edith Hall argues that tragedies tend to represent a world of 'extreme social heterogeneity and conflict ... tragedy offers a range of characters of all statuses from gods and kings to citizens and slaves'.[44] The result of this heterogeneity is to foreground debate and difference, 'transcending in fictive unreality the social limitations and historical conditions of [tragedy's] own production'.[45] Hall's argument is persuasive; nevertheless, it slightly

Euripides: Orestes

overemphasizes the inclusiveness and diversity of the cast of tragedy. It remains true that the main characters in the plays are all members of the ruling class. Even if we see tragedy as inherently democratic, it is still highly significant that there are comparatively few everyday characters who might be taken as representing 'normal' members of the public. There are plenty of minor figures such as servants, messengers, guards, soldiers, and so on, and there are from time to time lowly characters with a more prominent role (such as the Peasant in Euripides' *Electra*, or Phaedra's Nurse in *Hippolytus*); but in general the characters and their experiences are very far from those of the audience members.

Despite a few scattered references to 'the citizens' or 'the people of Athens' (etc.), tragedies usually give comparatively little impression of the *dêmos* as a collective body. It is sometimes thought that the chorus – the members of which are almost always of a lower social class than the main characters – function in some sense as an internalized representation of the citizen body, or (at least) as a significant collective presence which contrasts with the isolated aristocrats on stage.[46] However, the question of just what the chorus represent is a difficult one to answer. John Gould, notably, has argued that the type of 'collective identity' embodied by the chorus is very different from that of the democratic city-state and its discourse: he stresses instead the 'marginality' of most tragic choruses, who tend to be made up not of male citizens but of women, slaves, old men or barbarians.[47] The experiences of such people may well contrast with those of the aristocratic main characters, but they are also far removed from everyday civic life in fifth-century Athens. In *Orestes*, for example, it would take quite a big interpretative leap to see the chorus of female palace servants as somehow representing the entire population of either Argos or Athens.

But in *Orestes*, at any rate, it is clear that the chorus is not there to act as a *dêmos*-substitute, because here, unlike in most other tragedies, the population *as a whole* forms a distinct presence, separate from the chorus. Not only do 'the citizens of

5. Politics

Argos' play an unusually large part in the action, but they are also described in a strikingly pejorative manner. They are regarded as a discontented, volatile, aggressive mob, utterly opposed to the ruling family but also split by internal faction and conflicting interests. Throughout the play, 'the people' are always there, silently and invisibly, behind the scenes; they are a constant and distinctly menacing presence. The fact that they never actually appear (except for the mob who accompany Menelaus in the final scene, 1621-4), but are spoken about in the background, somehow increases the sense of their malignity and power over events.

Previous dramatizations of the myth had concentrated mainly on deeds and relationships *within* the royal palace. But now the action has been thrown open to outsiders, and family problems have become entwined with broader political problems. It seems now that everything is in the hands of the public: it is they who will decide the question of Clytemnestra's guilt or innocence (27); they who will 'permit' Orestes to hold the sceptre or take it away from him (437-8). We learn in the prologue (48-50) that the popular assembly is about to meet: officially its purpose is to decide the fate of Orestes and Electra, but it is clear that the decision to kill them is already as good as made (731).

As the play goes on, it gradually – and chillingly – becomes apparent that the characters in the palace are surrounded on all sides by fully armed men: it is stressed that not just a few people but the entire citizen body is implicated in this sinister action (446). There are guards posted on all sides; armed men patrol the streets; every road is blocked (760-2). The Argive women in the chorus have been made so nervous and jumpy by this state of affairs that they imagine they are about to be ambushed, even when there is actually no one there (1269-70, 1289-90). It is an intensely fraught and frightening situation (and, again, one can draw parallels with Thucydides' description of life at Athens in 411-410).

Towards the end of the prologue we see the effect of this situation on Helen, as she reveals that she wants to take ritual offerings to Clytemnestra's tomb but cannot do so, since she is

Euripides: Orestes

afraid to go out in front of the people (102). Electra, though she is far from sympathetic to Helen, agrees that there is 'something dreadful in the way that voices are being raised in Argos' (103). A little later, Helen instructs her daughter Hermione to go to the tomb on her behalf, bearing the message that Helen 'goes in terror of the Argive mob' (118-19). Helen, as we know only too well, is a common hate-figure in tragedy and elsewhere, but here the sense of her own guilt is outweighed by the far greater sense of the danger of the Argive population. It is not just Helen who fears the mob.

Often 'the people' are spoken of as an undifferentiated mob, but (as we have seen) it is made clear that there are distinct factions within the population: this increases the threat which they pose, since the whole community is seen as unstable. For instance, when Orestes is explaining to Menelaus that he is 'hated' by the public (428), he elaborates on this by saying that particular groups are after his blood. There is a certain Oeax, who has a grudge against Agamemnon and his family on account of the Trojan War (432), but there are also certain anonymous friends and supporters of Aegisthus, who (according to Orestes) exert a malign and powerful influence on others: 'it is they who have the ear of the city nowadays' (436). This sense of factional rivalry and impending schism is seen particularly in the assembly-scene (see above).

Elsewhere the Argive people are discussed in generic terms which may be taken as referring to mobs, or democracies, as a whole. Such lines can certainly be read as applying to the Athenian *dêmos* of 408, should we wish to interpret them along these lines. For instance, Menelaus tells Orestes that the Argives will be impossible to defeat in battle (696-701):

> for whenever the population of a city becomes angry and is passionate, it is like trying to extinguish a raging inferno; but if one calmly takes the strain and goes along with it, gauging the timing correctly, it may well blow itself out – and whenever it dies down, it is easy to take what you want from it.

5. Politics

This general advice combines anti-democratic sentiment with cynical opportunism: it is hard to say whether it reflects most badly on the public, on demagogic politicians, or on Menelaus himself. As one commentator writes, controversially, 'this passage doubtless gives the results of Euripides' own observation of the Athenian democracy'.[48] There *is* (as we have seen) room for doubt about Euripides' own views of democracy, but at the same time this passage does chime in with other contemporary writers' critical observations on late fifth-century Athenian politics, including Thucydides and the 'Old Oligarch'; one might even compare the fourth-century writer Plato's later criticisms of direct democracy as a political system (in such works as the *Republic* and *Laws*).

A similar gnomic reflection on the behaviour of democracies is seen a few lines later, in Orestes' exchange with Pylades when Menelaus has fled the scene. Pylades points out that the people do not have any legitimate power to punish him, but Orestes recognizes that, for right or wrong, they have so much power that they can do what they like: 'the masses are a frightening thing, especially when they have villainous leaders' (772). The word used for 'leaders' here (Greek *prostatai*) is the same word which Thucydides and other contemporary writers use of 'demagogues' such as Cleon, Hyperbolus and others.[49] It is also highly suggestive (whether or not he was right) that the ancient commentator on this passage detected an oblique reference to the politician Cleophon, who had played such a big part in the events of 411-409 BC.[50]

As we have seen, the messenger's report of the Argive assembly (866-956) contains very similar reflections on the unstable behaviour of the public. Once again, the fact that so much of his description is couched in general terms may lead us to contemplate its wide applicability as well as its specific relevance to Athens. Some editors have seen the political content as excessive or gratuitous, and several 'generic' lines have been deleted.[51] Perhaps later actors, producers or others were encouraged by the general tenor of Euripides' description to elaborate on the same anti-democratic themes.

Euripides: Orestes

Whatever the truth about that, it is safe to say that Euripides' description of the Argive/Athenian public is extraordinary by tragic standards. It is also a very far cry from the positive, even idealized, descriptions of the Athenian democracy which are encountered in earlier plays such as *Suppliant Women* and *Children of Heracles*.[52] Even if we did not know from other sources what had been happening at Athens since 411, we would take *Orestes* as a sign that things had changed for the worse.

At any rate – to return to the debate with which this chapter opened – there is nothing remotely *ideological* about this play's description of the people, or its implied view of the Argive (= Athenian) *polis*. We may choose to read the play as a specific comment on the degeneration of democracy in the last decade of the Peloponnesian War, or more generally as an 'anti-democratic' work (in the same tradition as contemporary writers such as the 'Old Oligarch' or Thucydides – though that is not how Euripides', or the other tragedians', political outlook is normally interpreted).[53] But condemnation (if that is what we are seeing here) is not restricted to the *dêmos* or to democracy: oligarchs and aristocrats also come in for criticism. No section of society and no individual or type emerges very well from all this.

To conclude the discussion, then: there is an unusually high amount of political content in *Orestes*. But essentially the play works in much the same way as any other Greek tragedy – by creating troubling, ambiguous, difficult-to-interpret parallels between myth and the real world. In this play, at least, no clear political message or meaning emerges. This lack of a 'message' is underlined by the fact that the problems in Argos are eventually resolved – after a fashion – not by political means but by supernatural intervention.[54] Nothing of the sort occurs in real life; and in any case the *deus ex machina* hardly offers a solution of a type that could be applied to the situation in Athens. There are no political lessons to be learnt from *Orestes*.

6

Euripides' Cleverest Play

The comic poet Strattis, at some point in the late fifth or early fourth century (perhaps soon after 408), put on a play called *Anthroporestes*. Its strange title means something along the lines of 'Orestes the Human Being', and it is clear that it was a parody of Euripides' *Orestes*.[1] Unfortunately, little else is known about the play, and nothing survives of it except the title and a few tiny fragments. Nevertheless, Strattis' comedy is good evidence for the history of the reception of *Orestes* within antiquity. Euripides' play must have caused quite a stir among its contemporary audiences for the comic poet to parody it at length: we might compare the impact of his *Helen* and other plays of 412, which inspired Aristophanes' comedy *Women at the Thesmophoria* in the following year.[2]

One of the fragments of *Anthroporestes* (fr. 1) is particularly revealing, because there Strattis or one of his characters described *Orestes* as Euripides' 'cleverest play' (*dexiôtaton drama* in Greek). This description is very significant. The word *dexios* ('clever'), like the nearly synonymous word *sophos*, is a term of apparent approbation, used by several ancient comedians to denote a certain type of sophistication, originality or dazzling inventiveness.[3] But the fact that this is comedy means that we can never be sure quite how seriously to take such descriptions. Are they jokes of some sort? Are they ironical? Aristophanes, for example, refers to himself as being *dexios* and *sophos*,[4] but he also uses exactly the same words, ironically, of Euripides, seemingly disparaging him for his meaningless paradoxes and verbal 'waffle'.[5] Socrates, too, is called *dexios* and *sophos* in

115

Euripides: Orestes

comedies which are savagely satirical about his intellectual pretensions.[6]

The word 'clever' in modern English usage is similarly ambiguous, since it can be used as a term of either praise or blame (perhaps reflecting an uncomfortable mixture of awe and envy in the user). 'Clever' may be used in a wholly positive sense, but often it is applied to something we admire without really liking; it frequently implies that the thing in question is too clever for its own good. Since comedy is always basically critical of its subject-matter, it is usual to interpret these labels in an ironical or negative sense: it is very likely that Strattis in *Anthroporestes* was putting the boot in, rather than paying homage to Euripides. But his description *dexiôtaton drama* is less important as an evaluative judgement than as a sign that *Orestes* and its 'clever' author were firmly associated with the ultra-sophisticated avant-garde movement in literature and thought.

Strattis is not alone in recognizing Euripides' cleverness. It has long been seen that Euripides' plays exhibit an overt preoccupation with intellectual or philosophical themes (perhaps more so than the work of other fifth-century dramatists). In antiquity he was frequently called 'the philosopher of the stage', and his name was connected with other prominent philosophers, including Socrates.[7] Furthermore, the period in which Euripides was writing has always been recognized as a particularly exciting time in the growth of new ideas. We have already seen, in previous chapters, that drama itself was becoming more innovative (in terms of its plots, use of myth, staging, music, rhythm and other aspects). But all these literary innovations must be seen against a background of astonishing intellectual developments – ideas about philosophy, science, language and knowledge were undergoing rapid transformation.

In particular, Euripides is often seen in the light of the so-called 'sophistic movement' which swept Athens in the last few decades of the fifth century.[8] The 'sophists' – whose number included Protagoras, Prodicus, Gorgias and Antiphon – were a new breed of philosopher and rhetorician, who shook up tradi-

6. Euripides' Cleverest Play

tional ways of thinking with their often radical ideas and caused controversy by charging money for teaching 'wisdom'. Their ideas included the notion that virtue could be taught; that moral values (or even reality itself) may be relative rather than absolute; that reality may not correspond to our perceptions of it; that language and rhetoric have an autonomous power of their own, independent of reality; and that on any topic at all there can be two completely opposite arguments. Most of these ideas have now become so fully integrated into everyday discourse that they can seem either obvious or banal, but it is clear that they had a powerful effect on those who were being exposed to them for the first time.

As well as the sophists, other intellectuals also had an obvious influence on Euripides and his contemporaries. We saw in Chapter 3 that Euripides' portrayal of Orestes' mental state may owe something to the theories of Hippocratic medicine. And as we shall see below, Presocratic philosophers such as Heraclitus of Ephesus, Anaxagoras of Clazomenae, and Empedocles of Acragas, with their speculations about cosmology and natural science, are also important (in some sense) for understanding the play.

This chapter, following the lead of Strattis, tries to relate *Orestes* to its intellectual context, showing that the play is conceptually inventive in all sorts of ways – including not just philosophical allusions but other types of 'cleverness' as well. But as we shall see, critics have disagreed about how to interpret all these allusions and ideas. Whether Euripides was writing to amuse his audience, to flatter their intelligence, to give them a demonstration of his own cleverness – or to stimulate them to serious philosophical thought – is a much-debated question.

Is Euripides *seriously* clever?

I have always found it surprising that modern scholars tend to see Euripides not as a serious intellectual but as a flashy, pretentious poseur who merely plays about with sophisticated ideas in a superficial way. (Thankfully, Socrates, who comes in for similar treatment in comedy, is not now dismissed in the same manner.[9]) This is the view taken by Desmond Conacher in his recent book *Euripides and the Sophists*, but it was expressed most forcefully by R.P. Winnington-Ingram in his well-known article 'Euripides: *poiêtês sophos*'.[10] According to Winnington-Ingram, 'despite this top-dressing of philosophy, Euripides was the least philosophic of the three tragedians'; rather, he was 'a sophisticated writer, addressing himself to other sophisticated persons, having and giving sophisticated fun'.[11]

Is Euripides serious or not? Even if *Orestes* is having 'fun' with philosophy, it is 'fun' of a rather different type from (say) Aristophanes' comedy *Clouds*, which pokes fun indiscriminately at Socrates, the sophistic movement, modern science and all sorts of other ideas which it mangles and distorts out of all recognition. But the question opens up a much broader discussion about the nature of tragedy and its relationship to philosophy. Unless we believe (as Nietzsche did) that drama and philosophy ought to be seen as inherently separate entities,[12] it seems perfectly normal to suppose that tragedy, like any sort of literature, can – sometimes – be a medium for genuine, profound philosophical enquiry. Euripides can – sometimes – be seen as a 'philosopher of the stage' in a literal sense. Indeed, there are tragedies in which the philosophical ideas seem to be so thoroughly worked into the plot, and explored with such depth and rigour, that the plays really do constitute a sustained, coherent treatment of those ideas. This is demonstrably true (for example) in the case of the 'escape-tragedies' *Helen*, *Andromeda* and *Iphigenia among the Taurians*, which have original things to say about the nature of reality and the problems inherent in language and sense-perception.[13]

But, at the same time (and at the risk of labouring this important point), tragedy is a very heterogeneous genre, and we need not assume that Euripides *always* wrote his plays in order to explore philosophical problems in depth. As we have already seen, *Orestes* is a notoriously difficult play to pin down to any

6. Euripides' Cleverest Play

sort of definitive interpretation (not just in a philosophical sense). As the next sections will show, it is comparatively easy to detect allusions in the play to various strands of contemporary thought, but it is much harder to join up all these strands into anything resembling a coherent philosophical argument.

Perhaps, then, Winnington-Ingram and the majority of critics are right to say that *Orestes* is only intended to provide sophisticated fun. But if we are inclined to be sceptical of this general approach, it is possible to take a different view. We can assume, instead, that there *is* a coherence in the play which we cannot grasp; that we are simply missing the point, owing to our own stupidity or to our lack of precise knowledge about what people like Anaxagoras actually thought and wrote. Alternatively, we might assume that Euripides is deliberately trying to confuse us, by throwing together allusions to concepts which collectively add up to nothing but leave the audience thoroughly baffled. But it may be helpful if we try to think specifically in terms of the play's effect on its original audience. On balance it seems likely that the play was designed to work on more than one level with regard to its numerous and diverse spectators. Some of them would no doubt have been serious intellectuals engaged with current thinking, some of them would have been well enough informed to catch at least some if not all the allusions, while many more of them would have been less well educated yet still able to enjoy the play and appreciate its sophistication.

Cleverness, metatheatricality and the play's 'tone'

Nevertheless, Winnington-Ingram's use of the word *fun* shows that there is another issue at stake here besides that of Euripides' intellectualism. Should tragedy be 'fun'? Should tragedy deal with 'clever' ideas? Is the 'tone' of *Orestes* suitable for a tragedy? This sort of question brings us back to the important point I made when discussing the play's critical reception in Chapter 1: the question of the play's *genre* continues to affect the way it has been interpreted.

Winnington-Ingram, like many others, sees Euripides as an

experimenter with genre; perhaps his aim in writing 'clever' plays like *Orestes* should be seen as not quite tragic but as more akin to comedy. I have already explained just why *Orestes* would not have been seen by its original audience as anything *but* a tragedy. Nevertheless, it is significant that many readers have detected something unusual about the mood of *Orestes*. Precisely at those moments when Euripides is being 'clever' there is often a tangible alteration in the tone of the play (or scene, or line) – a change which can be hard to describe or interpret. This change of tone amounts to a sort of exaggerated self-consciousness, almost as if Euripides' characters are stepping out of character and saying to the audience: 'Look at this!'

Critics sometimes use the term 'metatheatrical' to describe a certain type of self-consciousness in drama. This term denotes a range of self-referential techniques whereby the 'reality' of the dramatic situation is undermined, and it is made clear that the play *is* a play and the characters are really actors. Often this technique is used as a way of commenting on the conventions of theatre or the nature of the theatrical 'illusion'.[14] If we think that what Euripides is doing is essentially metatheatrical, it may help us to understand why many critics interpret his changes of tone as inherently *comic*. This is because Greek comedy very frequently 'breaks the illusion' and reminds its audience of its fictive status – so frequently, in fact, that this has been seen as one of the genre's defining characteristics (in contrast with tragedy).[15] Nevertheless, the *type* of metatheatricality that defines comedy is altogether brasher and more obvious. Comic characters talk, to the audience and to each other, about the theatre, stage-machinery, props, acting, playwrights and producers (and so on) in a way which completely undermines the 'illusion' and is far more exaggerated than anything we find in tragedy. Even Euripides at his most self-conscious (as in *Orestes*) is much more subtle than comedy in this respect.

Still, many people are uncomfortable with even tiny changes of tone in the context of tragedy.[16] If one sees tragedy as an intensely emotional genre, which relies for its power on evoking

6. Euripides' Cleverest Play

the audience's empathy for the characters, then perhaps even the slightest irony or distancing effect may seem out of place. But that would be a narrowly restrictive view of tragedy. Tragedy's tone, though it varies less than in comedy, is not constant: the plays contain a range of tonal effects. However, changes of tone are easier to detect than to interpret, and critics have struggled to find the right terminology to describe such effects. Labels such as 'comical', 'ludic', 'parodic', 'self-conscious', 'metatheatrical' (and so on) are often found in the secondary literature, but none is quite satisfactory, and in fact these terms all have quite distinct meanings.

It almost does not matter what terminology we use, so long as we realize that we are dealing with a species of *irony* (helpfully defined by one source as 'the use of language that has an inner meaning for a privileged audience and an outer meaning for the persons addressed or concerned').[17] Alterations of tone and self-conscious breaks in the 'illusion' are inherently ironical, and as such they contain a built-in ambivalence. In other words, we are dealing with precisely the sort of effect which, by its nature, is bound to divide readers. (Euripides' *spectators*, on the other hand, would have been given a few more clues to the meaning of the irony – they could listen to the actors' tone of voice and watch their mannerisms – but it is still unlikely that they would have been able to agree on an exact interpretation of the play's changes of tone.)

A few examples will illustrate some of the changes of tone in *Orestes* and some of the difficulties involved in describing just what effect is being created. For instance, there is an ironic variation of tone at lines 233-4, where Electra helps her brother raise himself from his sick-bed. 'Would you like me to set your feet down on the ground?' she asks him. 'It is a long time since you made a footprint – and change is always a pleasant thing.' Again (like various other lines spoken by Electra in the course of the play, from her unusual prologue-speech onwards), this seems a strange utterance: it does not quite make sense in the context, and so one suspects an additional meaning underlying her words.

Euripides: Orestes

Electra's gnomic comment about change (*metabolê*) has been interpreted as a 'clever' allusion to Heraclitus' philosophy of perpetual change and renewal. West even suggests that there may be a reference to a specific fragment of Heraclitus (fr. 56, 'it [the cosmic fire?] finds relief by changing').[18] If so, it is hard to see just why Heraclitus' theories should be alluded to at this point, and no one has succeeded in linking this allusion to any bigger argument at work in the play. Either we must concede that this is just a superficial allusion for the amusement of those in the know, or we must accept that there is some level of significance here that we are not in a position to grasp.

However, Electra's strange remark seems to have an additional (perhaps more intellectually satisfying) level of meaning if interpreted as a different sort of 'cleverness' altogether. I suggest that the mention of *footprints* would have rung a bell in the minds of most audience members, and that it is actually a reference to the notorious recognition-scene in Aeschylus' *Libation-Bearers* (205-28), in which Electra recognized her long-lost brother by the unlikely means of comparing his footprints to her own. In *Electra*, Euripides' own retelling of the same events, this unrealistic Aeschylean scene is implicitly criticized, as Electra is made to say that a brother and sister could not possibly be expected to have matching footprints (*Electra* 532-7).[19] It seems likely that Electra's incongruous mention of 'footprints' at *Orestes* 233-4 constitutes another self-conscious allusion to *Libation-Bearers* and also to *Electra* (which almost certainly predates *Orestes*). In this case, the word 'change' might not simply signal a reference to cosmological thought, but also emphasizes Euripides' own inventive approach to myth and narrative, adding a further level of complexity. Euripides is reminding us, as at other points in the play, that he has changed the details of the Orestes story in order to improve on Aeschylus' version.

Self-quotation by Euripides can also provide an explanation for the change of tone at 1520-2, where an odd joke (if that is what it is) intrudes into the scene of dialogue between the murderous Orestes and the terrified Phrygian slave:

6. Euripides' Cleverest Play

Phrygian: Keep your sword away from me: at this range it has a terrible, murderous glint.
Orestes: Surely you aren't afraid of turning into stone, as if you had glimpsed the Gorgon?
Phrygian: No, I'm afraid of turning into a corpse; I've never heard of the Gorgon's head.

The ancient commentator found these lines unacceptably 'comical and pedestrian', and his distaste has been echoed by certain modern editors, who delete parts of this scene of dialogue.[20] But (even if the lines are interpolated) it is worth asking exactly what is going on in this scene. The reference to the Gorgon (the snake-haired monster slain by Perseus) seems out of context, and the dialogue contains a marked *non sequitur*. Orestes never mentioned the Gorgon's *head*, so when the Phrygian says that he has 'never heard of the Gorgon's head', his supposed ignorance cannot be taken at face value. Why mention the Gorgon at all? It is very probably an allusion to Euripides' own play, *Andromeda*, in which the Gorgon's head, severed by the hero Perseus and carried around with him in his bag, played a prominent role.[21] Since *Orestes* (as we have seen in earlier chapters) frequently refers back to Euripides' *Helen*, it is perfectly plausible that it should contain references to Euripides' other works as well (and even more likely, perhaps, that it should allude to a play staged in the same year as *Helen*). But it is difficult to go further than merely noting the allusion: it may have had a deeper meaning that we cannot see, or it may simply be an in-joke for Euripides' fans in the form of an amusing reference to be noted.

Another comparable moment, which relies for its effect specifically on the audience's knowledge of earlier tragedies, is seen towards the end of the play, when Menelaus confronts the men who are threatening his daughter (1591-2):

Menelaus: And you, Pylades – are you also taking part in this killing?
Orestes: He says yes silently. It will suffice if I do the talking.

123

Euripides: Orestes

As Winnington-Ingram recognized, these lines break the 'illusion': that is to say, 'there is no dramatic necessity for this question to be asked nor is any dramatic purpose served by it. It is completely gratuitous.' He sees it, I think rightly, as a self-conscious reference to the 'three-actor' rule (there are now so many actors on stage that Pylades' part must be played by a mute).[22] Malcolm Davies goes even further, and detects a specific cross-reference to the astonishing scene in Aeschylus' *Libation-Bearers* (899-903) in which the previously mute character Pylades suddenly speaks three lines.[23] The scene in *Orestes* is thus a 'mirror-image' of the Aeschylean scene, and the point is intertextual (Euripides is appealing to his audience's detailed knowledge of earlier literary works) rather than merely a comment on theatrical conventions in general. But is it a joke? Is the tone of this 'clever' scene comparable to comedy? Opinions are bound to differ.

What's new in Argos?

The scenes discussed above all seem to exhibit one type of 'cleverness' in particular. That is, Euripides can be seen as using these ironical changes of tone in order to draw attention to his own poetic originality: he is prompting the spectators to recall his own earlier triumphs or his rival tragedians' efforts. This sort of effect is often called 'metatheatrical',[24] even though Euripides is not actually drawing attention to his play's theatricality as such. As recent scholars have made clear, it is very hard to find examples of true 'metatheatricality' in fifth-century tragedy (as opposed to comedy).[25] When discussing Euripidean self-consciousness in these passages, it would be more accurate to talk of 'intertextuality', the term generally used to denote an author's highly self-conscious knowledge and awareness of the relationship between literary texts. Euripides, in common with most other writers (of any genre or period), is concerned to highlight his own individual qualities in relation to his predecessors. This may well be 'clever', but once again whether we find this sort of thing

6. Euripides' Cleverest Play

'fun' or 'funny' will depend on how we view the business of intertextuality as a whole.

As we have already seen, the plot of *Orestes* and its presentation of the situation in Argos differs strikingly from earlier works on the same theme (such as Stesichorus' or Aeschylus' *Oresteia*, Sophocles' *Electra* and others). At a number of points throughout the play Euripides seems to be deliberately reminding us of the fact that most of the plot is his own invention. It is particularly interesting to note that the characters use the Greek word *kainos* ('new' or 'strange') to describe what is happening around them. Even though this was a common enough adjective in Greek, the characters use it more often than one would expect, and in a way that makes us suspect that its meaning is somehow marked.

It seems that *kainos* became something of a 'buzz-word' in late fifth-century Athens, used by and of radical innovators in poetry, drama and music. Timotheus, for instance, used the word to describe his 'New Musical' style and contrast it with outdated older music.[26] Aristophanes called his own work *kainos*, but also, notoriously, used the word to refer to Euripides' revision of the Helen myth.[27] When Euripides' characters go out of their way to refer to the 'novelty' of the events in the play, it is not hard to detect an ironical change in tone. (In fact, Euripides himself uses the word *kainos* considerably more than any other extant fifth-century writer – a highly suggestive fact.)

The first mention of 'novelty' comes at the beginning of the first episode, just after Orestes has awoken from slumber. Electra tells her brother to listen, since she has something to tell him. 'You're going to tell me something new (*kainon*),' he replies (239). Now *kainon* here could be taken in an unmarked sense, or (as Willink observes) it might connote something 'unwelcome', but since it comes immediately after the ironical mention of footprints (234), and since everything that has so far happened in the play is indeed strangely new, one suspects that there is an extra, underlying meaning. And, as it transpires, the news that Electra wants to tell Orestes does mark a distinct

Euripides: Orestes

change from the usual myth: Menelaus has arrived, with his fleet, in Nauplia (241-2).

As the play continues, yet more oddities and innovations are introduced into the plot. At one point, as Orestes and Pylades discuss how they will behave in front of the Argive assembly (790), Orestes starts to say: 'Only one obstacle stands in my way ...', but Pylades interrupts him, asking: 'What is this latest new development (*kainon*)?' (790). The tone of this question, again, seems obviously ironical (what? – not *another* invented detail, on top of all the others?). When, a few lines later on, the Messenger turns to one of the citizens in the assembly and asks him 'What's new (*kainon*) in Argos?' (875), the answer might well be: pretty much *everything*. Euripides' Argos is *so* unfamiliar that these reminders of its strangeness are almost unnecessary.

When, in the midst of all this, the chorus sing about the unpredictability of life ('Behold how fate determines everything contrary to expectations!' 977-8), it is hard not to see their seemingly gnomic generalization as another self-referential comment on the twists in the plot. This is hinted at by West, who comments: 'the idea is naturally emphasized by a dramatist who deals in surprises, and we should bear in mind that the chorus' and the audience's present expectations are still to be upset'.[28] The chorus take on this ironical function even more explicitly in the final scene of the play, when Orestes comes face-to-face with the bizarre Phrygian slave. 'And now look at this!' they chant, 'here is novelty upon novelty' (*kainon ek kainôn tode*, 1503) – a brilliant opening to the eventful (and completely invented) final scene which follows.

Myth, illusion and reality

Nevertheless, we should not invariably see each 'clever' change of tone as a nod to Euripides' own originality and sophistication. There may sometimes be an additional, deeper meaning to be found. This observation leads us back to the specifically *philosophical* content of *Orestes*, as opposed to the other varieties of 'cleverness' that we have seen in the play.

6. Euripides' Cleverest Play

In this respect, it is worth having a second look at Electra's extraordinary prologue-speech. In this speech, as we have already seen (pp. 25-8 above), she simultaneously creates *and* destroys the dramatic 'illusion'. At the same time as she is establishing the play's plot and characters, she also maintains a distinctly ironical distance from everything she describes. Electra seems to know that she and her relatives are characters in a myth which is already well known to the audience (14, 16-17, 27, 30, etc.); she refers to the characters as being 'famous' (17, 21); she prefaces her accounts of family history – which contain unusual or made-up details – with sceptical-sounding phrases such as *'so they say'* (5, 8) ... and so on. As we have already argued in Chapter 1, this detached tone can make it difficult for us to engage fully with Electra as a real character: in some senses she can strike us more as an impartial observer than as a participant in the events. Since she actually addresses the audience in a couple of places (27, 128-9), an effect which is not seen elsewhere in extant tragedy, this scene represents a very extreme rupturing of the 'illusion'.

This time the cleverness is not of an intertextual sort: as far as we can tell, there is no reference being made here to any specific works of earlier literature. Nor is it metatheatrical, since once again it is not the *theatricality* of the events that is being emphasized. Instead, it is myth and the mythical tradition (as such) that are under the microscope. What we have, then, if we want to give it a label, is really 'metamythological'. Euripides can be seen as using this technique to problematize the concept of myth itself. More specifically, he is undermining the *reality* of the myths under discussion.

If we are to engage with the play at all, we have to suspend our disbelief for the duration of the viewing or reading experience, and so we conventionally treat its events as 'real' in a strictly limited sense. But for Euripides' audience these myths were 'real' in a more literal sense. Greek myths were virtually indistinguishable from history; they were the basis of Greek religious and ritual practices; they were crucial in establishing one's sense of personal, local and national identity – the Greeks *believed* in their myths, to a large (if not total) extent.[29] But *Orestes*, in its prologue and elsewhere, seems to be suggesting that one cannot entirely believe in myths; that in fact the relationship between myths and reality is questionable.

This sceptical attitude to myth is sometimes seen as just another facet of its author's superficial wit, but it may be interpreted as having more serious philosophical consequences. As I mentioned above, the sophists' views about language and reality seem to be important for understanding the play. The influence of one sophist in particular, Gorgias of Leontini, looms large in Euripides' work. Gorgias was particularly interested in questions of ontology and epistemology – that is, in the nature of reality and the extent to which anyone can ever truly know anything about it. In his most famous work, *On Not-Being* (or *On Nature*), Gorgias argued three propositions: first, that nothing exists; second, that even if it did, we have no reliable way of apprehending it with our senses; and third, that even if we could apprehend reality, we would not be able to communicate it adequately to anyone else through language.[30] In other words, sense-perception and language are essentially forms of illusion or delusion: even though they are the only clues we possess as to the nature of the world, they do not correspond to reality at all. This drastically negative outlook has been interpreted as a sort of 'philosophical nihilism'.[31]

Euripides had already absorbed these ideas into his *Helen* (which is also an implicit response to Gorgias' famous work about the same character, the *Encomium of Helen*).[32] This tragedy thoroughly explores the mismatch between appearances and reality, most notably through the motif of Helen's phantom-double; and it makes the crucial point that *myths* are, like appearances and words of all kinds, just another species of illusion. I have already argued that *Orestes* was conceived as a 'sequel' to *Helen*, and now its relationship to the earlier play can be understood on the philosophical level as well. (It will be increasingly clear to the reader that in order to appreciate *Orestes* fully it is necessary to read *Helen* first!) Both plays seem to be raising much the same type of

6. Euripides' Cleverest Play

unsettling doubts about whether anything in front of us is real or not.

The appearance, early on in *Orestes*, of the 'same old Helen' (129) would immediately have made the audience recall the earlier tragedy and its intellectual themes. In particular, it would have caused them to wonder if this Helen is any more real than the other one: who *is* the real Helen? As the play moves forward, the disparity between reality and illusion, seeming and being, words and real objects (etc.) is emphasized repeatedly, as it was in *Helen*, by a number of scenes of self-conscious and paradoxical word-play. For instance (to take a few examples more or less at random), Orestes tells Electra, curiously, that it is more important to *seem* healthy than to be healthy ('the illusion is better, even if it falls short of the truth', 235-6); later Orestes *thinks* he sees the Furies, but it is a delusion (259), and he fights them with an imaginary bow and arrow (271-7); Apollo is said to have encouraged Orestes not in *reality* but *in word* only (286-7); Orestes is said to be both dead *and* alive (385-6); he claims that his *name* lives on, even though his *body* is withered (390), and criticizes those who are friends *in name* but not in *reality* (454-5); it is claimed that Orestes, in killing his mother, was simultaneously 'wrong (*anosios*) and right (*hosios*), calling it by an alternative *name*' (546-7) ... and so on.[33] The cumulative effect of all this word-play is to undermine the reality of everything before our eyes (and also, by extension, our notions of reality in general). What we see in front of us, and what we say about it, may have nothing to do with reality at all.

Our attempts to understand the awful events in Argos will become even more difficult, if everything in the play – or the whole world – is revealed to be either illusory or delusory. All that one will be able to conclude, perhaps, is that the world is hopelessly confusing. Even if one is not prepared to go to such nihilistic extremes, it is obvious that all these doubts about the reliability of myth and the capacity of human knowledge impinge upon the central moral questions of the play. Did Agamemnon and Clytemnestra deserve to die? Are Pylades and

Euripides: Orestes

Orestes right to try to murder Helen? These questions had been difficult enough to answer in previous versions of the myth, but now they are complicated yet further by the thought that we cannot even know or adequately communicate what really happened. What are we to think? Electra, strikingly, leaves it up to the public to decide (27): she is acknowledging that there is a degree of moral relativity involved in judging these issues, but also implying that they are ultimately impossible to resolve – or even (perhaps) that it does not matter very much.

The ethical problems are summed up succinctly in the conversation between Orestes and Pylades, as they deliberate whether to stay and face the Argive assembly. Orestes says: 'At any rate, the *fact* is that I have justice on my side'. Pylades replies: 'Just pray that you *seem* to have justice' (782).[34] Some readers find Pylades' response chillingly amoral. But perhaps, given the difficulties inherent in apprehending the reality of the situation, the *semblance* of justice is all that can ever be hoped for.

Sophistic rhetoric and the *agôn*

The sophists' most important contribution to Athenian life probably consisted of the new modes of argumentation which they popularized. It is clear that the Athenians became obsessed with rhetoric during the last two or three decades of the century, and that the speeches heard in the assembly and the law-courts were more elaborately crafted than ever before. The comedies of the period are a good sign of this popular craze: for example, the plot of Aristophanes' *Clouds* (produced in 423) is based on a young man learning rhetoric in order to evade his creditors, and it features the Just and the Unjust Argument among its cast of characters. The next year Aristophanes wrote another comedy, *Wasps*, in which an old man becomes so seriously fixated with listening to law-court speeches that his son has to lock him in his bedroom. The historian Thucydides, reporting a famous speech which Cleon delivered before the Athenian assembly in 427 BC, makes the politician criticize the Athenians for acting more like an 'audience' than a political

6. Euripides' Cleverest Play

assembly: they have, he says, become victims of their own pleasure in listening to clever debates.

The increasing frequency of *agôn*-scenes in tragedy at this period is a sign of how popular rhetorical debates had become. The *agôn* is a forensic-style confrontation between two of the main characters, who represent, as it were, the 'defence' *versus* the 'prosecution'. Neither party 'wins' the case. As often noted, these highly unrealistic and stylized scenes never have any effect on the plot, and they could be removed without anyone really noticing. Obviously *agônes* provided an opportunity for the playwright to entertain his audience with a rhetorical display of the type they so enjoyed, but they have another function too, in that they seem to sum up some of the main themes of the plot and the motivations of the characters.[35]

Like some of the other ideas mentioned above, many of the sophists' figures of speech and rhetorical tricks are nowadays so familiar that they seem unremarkable, but we have to try to imagine their effect on an audience who had never used language in quite this way before. These revolutionary devices included the argument from *eikos* (probability); the argument from *êthos* (character); the hypothetical syllogism ('if *x* were the case, then ...'); *hypophora* (the classic rhetorical question: 'Is the Pope Catholic?'); *prokatalêpsis* (anticipating your opponent's main points and disproving them in advance); *antikatêgoria* (accusing your accuser); *adynaton* (mentioning an impossibility); *reductio ad absurdum* (taking an argument to ridiculous extremes), and so on.[36] Armed with such an array of rhetorical devices, so the sophists claimed, anyone could win any argument on any topic.

The *agôn* between Orestes and Tyndareus (491-604) is highly rhetorical in form. We have already mentioned the *content* of their speeches,[37] but the *style* of argumentation is as important as the arguments themselves. The debate begins, self-consciously, by announcing itself as such: Tyndareus calls it 'an *agôn* of intelligence' (491).[38] He proceeds to introduce a number of hypothetical syllogisms: *if* right and wrong are obvious to everyone, there is no need for an *agôn* at all (491-2), and *if*

Euripides: Orestes

Orestes had sent Clytemnestra into exile, he would have been a righteous and just man – but as it is, he is guilty (499-504). A similar figure is used at 508-18, combined with *reductio ad absurdum*, as Tyndareus asks what the logical outcome will be if one murder is committed in revenge for every previous murder: there will always be someone with blood on his hands until there is no one left. Several times Tyndareus appeals to the law (*nomos*, 503, 523; cf. 500), though it is in fact far from clear what laws would have been in place in the 'Argos' (Athens?) of the play. The speech ends, after a couple of rhetorical questions (526-8, 532-3) and a legalistic appeal to 'witnesses' (533), with Tyndareus' recommendation that Orestes should pay the penalty of death.

The chorus (as usual in *agônes*) speak a couple of conventional lines (542-3) separating the two speeches, and then Orestes makes his defence. He starts off (544-50) with a flattering and respectful reference to his grandfather's age and wisdom (a tactic called *captatio benevolentiae*). Next he, too, makes appeal to the law (*nomos*), but he admits – in a typically sophistic paradox – that he was both inside and outside the law, depending on what *name* one chooses to use (546-7). *Hypophora* follows ('what *ought* I to have done?' 551), then the argument from *êthos*, as the moral character of Clytemnestra and Aegisthus is criticized (557-63).

Orestes' next argument is extremely bold: he claims that he should be seen not as a criminal but as the benefactor of all Greece, because by killing Clytemnestra he has put a stop to the 'general practice' – also called *nomos* in Greek – of wives murdering their husbands (564-71). On the one hand, this is a clever reversal of the charge, making his 'crime' seem to be a good deed and giving a completely different meaning to the word *nomos*. On the other hand, it is such a far-fetched argument that it almost comes across as a *reductio ad absurdum* – the figure which he ought to have used in undermining Tyndareus' arguments, not in ruining his own case!

Following this, Orestes returns to the *êthos* of Clytemnestra and her own crimes (573-8), adding that justice (573) is on his side, not hers. At 578 Orestes swears an oath by the gods, which

6. Euripides' Cleverest Play

is an emphatic technique but often a sign of desperation; he weakens its impact by admitting that it is an ill-omened thing to mention the gods during a murder trial (579-80). More rhetorical questions are posed (581-4): what would Agamemnon's spirit have done if Orestes had *not* avenged him? Finally, Orestes turns to the device of *antikatêgoria*, naming first Tyndareus (585) and then Apollo (591) as the truly guilty parties, before ending (596-9) with more *hypophora* in a 'rising tricolon' figure (i.e. three rhetorical questions, each longer than the last). A short quarrel between the speakers then takes place, but it is clear that the *agôn* has achieved nothing except to make both parties more resolute.

It is likely that Euripides' audience would have been highly entertained by this debate. Both speakers – whatever we may think of their opinions – employ an impressive range of argumentative tactics. Orestes' arguments are more varied, but somewhat less well chosen, than those of Tyndareus – perhaps appropriately, given his status as the guilty (and already condemned) party. However, one of the biggest problems in evaluating speeches of this sort is that the antagonists' arguments may not straightforwardly reflect their character or views. Perhaps this *agôn* merely represents rhetoric for the sake of rhetoric, and perhaps the opinions expressed so persuasively by Orestes and Tyndareus are just the sort of words that *could* be used by a clever speaker faced with the same situation. The *agôn* takes on a different light if we view it as, primarily, an exercise in rhetoric rather than a true statement of the speakers' moral positions. And, in any case, we must remember to read these sophisticated arguments in the light of the sophists' other views about language and knowledge, truth and illusion. These *words* may entertain us, or they may sway us in one direction or another – but do they have any connection at all to *reality*?

Cosmology

The sophists and their unsettling views are, as I said above, not the only intellectual influence on Euripides. It has often been pointed out that *Orestes* also contains a number of allusions to

Euripides: Orestes

Presocratic theories of cosmology. The first such allusion is seen in the first lines of the prologue (showing, once again, that Electra's prologue-speech has a markedly 'programmatic' function, clearly announcing the thematic preoccupations of the play). We are told that Electra's wicked ancestor Tantalus is 'suspended in mid-air, dreading a rock which hangs over his head' (6-7).

Even if no particular philosophical point were being made here, this description would immediately strike us as a peculiar divergence from the normal myth, since Tantalus *himself* (rather than just the rock) is seen as air-borne. What makes it even odder is that the description of Tantalus and the rock corresponds exactly to Anaxagoras' theory about the workings of the universe. The fragment quoted here outlines the philosopher's beliefs about the way in which heavenly bodies are suspended between heaven and earth by centrifugal motion in the ether:[39]

> Anaxagoras said that the earth is flat, and stays suspended because of its size, because there is no void, and because it is carried like a vessel by the air, which is extremely strong ... The sun, moon, and all the heavenly bodies are fiery stones which have been taken up by the rotation of the ether. Beneath the heavenly bodies are certain bodies, invisible to us, that are carried around along with the sun and moon.

Tantalus' rock corresponds to a meteorite in this Anaxagorean reworking of the myth, and Tantalus himself is in a similar state – a much stranger and more terrifying form of punishment than usual.

A more explicit visualization of Tantalus' position in the cosmos is found later in the play, when Electra (in a lyric aria) expresses the wish that she could soar up into space and visit Tantalus (982-5):

> Would that I could go to that rock suspended between sky

6. Euripides' Cleverest Play

and earth by golden chains, to the mass broken off from
Olympus, borne about by whirlwinds, so that I might raise
a cry of lamentation to my old ancestor ...

Again, this description matches up with various fragments of
Anaxagoras, but there are also elements which may owe something to other sources. A joke about 'whirlwinds' (*dinai* in
Greek) in Aristophanes' philosophical comedy *Clouds* hints at
the fact that these phenomena were an obsession of other
fifth-century intellectuals, while the additional detail of 'golden
chains' to represent the centrifugal forces in the ether (not seen
in the fragments of Anaxagoras) may be taken from elsewhere.[40] Ruth Scodel, in her perceptive discussion of these
passages, suggests that Euripides probably took the 'golden
chains' motif from a contemporary allegorical interpretation of
the myth, or from Homer, though the particular combination of
all these elements may well have been Euripides' own idea.[41]

As with all the other 'clever' ideas in the play, one can choose
to read these passages as no more than facile allusions to
contemporary science, but there may be more to it than that. It
has to be admitted that we know comparatively little about
Anaxagoras' ideas, apart from a few perplexing fragments, so
(once again) there may well be some meaning that we are
missing. But as it is, the cosmological perspective at least adds
nuance to the play's presentation of events at Argos: the problems of this one doomed family are now seen as possessing a
(literally) 'universal' significance. We already knew that certain
gods took an interest in the Tantalid line, but now the family
appears as part of an even wider context, as somehow being
inextricably caught up in the workings of the universe as a
whole.

Edith Hall has suggested another way of looking at the
cosmological ideas in the play. Rather than focusing on
Anaxagoras, she argues that the theories of Heraclitus and
Empedocles are relevant. Both of these cosmologists believed
that strife (Greek *eris*) was a controlling principle in the universe. Heraclitus wrote that everything owes its existence to

strife and necessity, and (a closely comparable idea) that war is the 'father' of all things. Empedocles, similarly, wrote that the universe – like human behaviour – is governed by the twin forces of love and strife.[42]

As Hall points out, these cosmic powers are apparently at work behind the recent doings in the house of Atreus. We have already seen how one principle, love, is exemplified in the relationship between Orestes, Pylades and Electra – which may have implicitly political overtones, if we see these 'friends' as a quasi-oligarchic club.[43] The other principle, strife, can be seen as being embodied in the political unrest which exists in Argos, but it is also explicitly named, either as an abstract noun or as a personification, at several prominent points in the play. The prologue, for instance (12-13), states that it was the goddess Strife who caused the brothers Atreus and Thyestes to quarrel; and Electra in her solo aria (1001-12) attributes her own suffering and all the family's problems to Strife, who is depicted as having made the sun and stars change course. In other words, Euripides is implying that there is a natural connection between cosmic, domestic and political disturbances in Argos.[44]

Hall's reading of *Orestes* is important because it is a convincing and satisfying attempt to link together the cosmological allusions and the play's broader concerns. In fact, the more we examine *all* these 'clever' ideas, the more it appears that they are thematically integrated into the play, rather than being pointless intrusions or a mere 'top-dressing of philosophy'. Most of Euripides' allusions to contemporary thought, even if they cannot always be completely understood by modern readers, are deeply connected with the other problems which the play explores. However, even if this is true, it does not mean that it is any easier to understand the play in terms of a coherent philosophical argument. Euripides may well have been a serious intellectual rather than a dabbler, but this play is still likely to leave us baffled.

In the end, it is just as hard to find a philosophical 'meaning' in *Orestes* as it was to identify any underlying political message in the play's events. As I have been trying to show throughout

6. Euripides' Cleverest Play

this book, *Orestes* does not lend itself to straightforward interpretations or easy answers to the questions which it raises. This intractability may elicit either admiration or frustration: it is up to us to decide. But whether or not we admire *Orestes,* and whether or not we feel any closer to *understanding* it as such, we can at least begin to appreciate what Euripides' first audience, on that spring day in 408, must have made of this difficult, clever, incongruous, ironical tragedy.

Notes

1. Setting the Scene

1. The ancient evidence relating to the festival and its organization can be found (in translation) in Csapo and Slater, *Context of Ancient Drama*, or (in Greek, with fuller discussion) in Pickard-Cambridge, *Dramatic Festivals of Athens*.
2. It is usually thought that playwrights after Aeschylus abandoned connected trilogies: see Pickard-Cambridge, *Dramatic Festivals of Athens*, pp. 80-1. Nevertheless, there is very little evidence one way or the other.
3. Kovacs, *Euripidea* usefully collects and translates all this biographical material.
4. Lefkowitz, *Lives of the Greek Poets*.
5. The issue of dating Euripides' plays is too complex to discuss here: see Collard, *Euripides* for a brief introduction.
6. A very good survey of 'typical' tragic plots is provided by Burian, 'Myth into *Mythos*'.
7. For two recent (and completely opposed) viewpoints, see Scullion, 'Tragedy Misconceived as Ritual', and Seaford, *Dionysus* and *Reciprocity and Ritual*.
8. For more discussion of the theatre and stagecraft, see Taplin, *Greek Tragedy in Action*, esp. ch. 1, and Wiles, *Greek Theatre Production*.
9. www.apgrd.ox.ac.uk.
10. This is remarked on by Fiona Macintosh, 'Tragedy in Performance', p. 320: she is referring to Laurence Boswell's production of *Agamemnon's Children* (a version of *Electra*, *Orestes* and *Iphigenia among the Taurians*) at the Gate Theatre in March 1995.
11. See Hall and Macintosh, *Greek Tragedy on the British Stage* (Index s.v. 'Orestes').
12. Comic parody of *Or.* includes Aristophanes, *Frogs* 303-4; Menander, *The Man from Sikyon* 176-85; Alexis fr. 3; Apollodorus fr. 6; Eubulus fr. 64; Nicolaus fr. 1; Sannyrion fr. 8.
13. Strattis fr. 1. I return to the question of the play's 'cleverness' in Chapter 6.

139

14. See Willink's commentary ad loc. For the inscriptions, see B. Snell, *Tragicorum Graecorum Fragmenta* (Gottingen: Vandenhoeck and Ruprecht, 1971), vol. i, DID A 2a; B 11.
15. See Page, *Actor's Interpolations*, especially pp. 41-55.
16. Translation taken from W. Jackson Knight's superb Penguin edition (Harmondsworth 1956), p. 111.
17. See Handley and Green, *Images of the Greek Theatre*, no. 71 (p. 97): this image of Electra tending the sick Orestes seems to be based on *Orestes* 233-315.
18. On the history of the text's transmission, see Willink's commentary (pp. lvii-lxiv) and, for a much fuller study, Diggle, *Textual Tradition*.
19. The opinions quoted are taken from: West's commentary, p. 28; Kovacs, *Euripides V*, pp. 405-8; Patin, *Etudes,* pp. 259-69; Reinhardt, 'Intellectual Crisis', p. 32; Kitto, *Greek Tragedy*, p. 346; Burnett, *Catastrophe Survived*, p. 183; Bates, *Euripides*, p. 167.
20. The nineteenth- and twentieth-century scholarship on *Or.* is conveniently summarized by Porter, *Studies*, pp. 1-44.
21. See also Chapter 4 below for Nietzsche's view of 'late Euripides'.
22. This last approach is exemplified by Dunn, 'Tragic and Comic License', Knox, 'Euripidean Comedy', Zeitlin, 'Closet of Masks', etc.
23. See Wright, *Escape-Tragedies*, p. 10.
24. On modern interpretations, and misinterpretations, of Aristotle see (e.g.) Halliwell, *Aristotle's Poetics*; Lucas, *Tragedy*, etc.
25. The 'murder', or *attempted* murder, of Helen, poses a problem: see Chapter 2 below.
26. On the possibility of humour in tragedy, and its functions, see Seidensticker, *Palintonos Harmonia*.
27. *Orestes* 1-7: see my discussion of the play's prologue below.
28. See Davies, *Epic Cycle* for discussion of these works.
29. The prologue as a device is studied by Erbse, *Studien zum Prolog*. No full-length study exists in English, but Goward, *Telling Tragedy*, pp. 1-26, has some valuable remarks. On the prologue of *Or.* in general, see Willink's commentary ad loc.
30. E.g. Taplin, 'A *Synkrisis*', pp. 165-73. Cf. Bain, *Actors and Audience*, pp. 1-12, 61.
31. See (for example) Easterling's sensible discussion in *The Cambridge Companion to Greek Tragedy*, pp. 165-8.
32. See Chapter 6 below for more about cosmology.

2. Dramatic Structure and Performance

1. On questions of staging and the limitations of the evidence, see, most recently, Davidson, 'Theatrical Production'. Cf. Taplin, *Greek Tragedy in Action*, pp. 1-21.
2. On the controversial question of the shape of the theatre, see the

Notes to pages 30-37

various contributions to Wilson, *Greek Theatre Rituals*, which deals *inter alia* with the latest archaeological surveys.

3. Ashby, *Classical Greek Theatre*, pp. 81-7, reproduces a number of artists' reconstructions of the *mêchanê*.

4. E.g. Aristophanes, *Women at the Thesmophoria* 1008-1132; *Peace* 79-179.

5. E.g. Schlegel, *Vorlesungen*, pp. 103-28, followed by most nineteenth-century German scholars: see Porter, *Studies*, pp. 4-11. Cf. (*inter alia*) Kitto, *Greek Tragedy* for the old-fashioned type of view (p. 332ff. deals with the supposed deficiencies of *Or.* in particular). More recently, Conacher, *Euripidean Drama*, p. 213, refers to 'several stages of related action', while di Benedetto in his edition of the play (on 1624-93) perceives a total lack of dramatic tension in the later scenes.

6. Heath's Penguin edition of *Poetics*, with its excellent Introduction, is a good starting-point for discussion of Aristotle's views on tragedy.

7. Grube, *Drama of Euripides*, p. 397.

8. Porter, *Studies*, pp. 45-54.

9. Burnett, *Catastrophe Survived*, esp. pp. 183-222 (on *Or.*).

10. Spira, *Untersuchungen*, pp. 113-38; Solmsen, 'Euripides' *Ion*'. Porter, *Studies* (pp. 96-9) adopts a similar, though more nuanced, reading of the play.

11. See Halleran, *Stagecraft*, pp. 41-2: *Ion* 1553 and *IA* 819, 855 are the only other surviving examples of 'false preparation'.

12. Scholion on line 57 (discussed by Willink in his commentary, p. 92 and Page, *Actors' Interpolations*, pp. 41-2).

13. Hartigan, *Greek Tragedy on the American Stage*, pp. 124-7.

14. Shared Experience Productions, directed by Nancy Meckler. The company's 'Education Pack' for *Orestes*, designed by Gillian King, is very helpful (available online at: sharedexperience.org.uk).

15. Ellen Beckerman's 2001 production at HERE Arts Center, New York, reviewed by Les Gutman in *Curtain Up*, 25th April 2001 (www.curtainup.com/orestes.html).

16. David Cote in *Time Out* (New York edition, 5-11 April, 2007).

17. Cf. the 'duet' form of the *parodos* in *Helen, Ion,* etc.

18. Kranz, *Stasimon*, pp. 240-1, discusses 'mimetic' effects in the New Music.

19. See Hartigan, *Greek Tragedy on the American Stage*, pp. 124-7; cf. Ellen Beckerman's 2004 New York production (described online at www.theatermania.com).

20. Christy Bigelow's production at Reed College, reviewed by Alison Hallett in the *Portland Mercury*, 12 October 2006.

21. See Aara Suski's review in *Didaskalia* 1.4 (1994): online at www.didaskalia.net.

22. Aristophanes, *Frogs* 303-4; Sannyrion fr. 8; Strattis frr. 1 and 60.

23. The music survives in a papyrus fragment of the second or third century BC (Vienna G 2315), edited and transcribed by Pöhlmann and West, *Documents of Ancient Greek Music*, pp. 12-17. See also West's commentary, pp. 203-4.

24. See West's commentary ad loc. Others treat the lines as genuine: cf. Halleran, *Stagecraft* p. 13.

25. Aristophanes, *Acharnians* 410-17.

26. See Duchemin, *L'agôn dans la tragédie grecque*, Lloyd, *The Agon in Euripides*, and Conacher, 'Rhetoric and Relevance'. I return to this scene in Chapter 6 below.

27. Walton, *Living Greek Theatre*, p. 368.

28. For most recent discussion, see West's commentary ad loc. (responding to Willink's substantial treatment). For my purposes here I accept West's text of lines 819-26, which is identical with Diggle's Oxford Classical Text.

29. See Alexiou, *The Ritual Lament in Greek Tradition*, pp. 131-4.

30. West's commentary, p. 255.

31. Willink's commentary, pp. 281-2.

32. Wright, *Escape-Tragedies*, ch. 2, discusses Euripides' treatment of myth in *Helen*, which seems to constitute a mixture of mythical variants rather than the outright invention of material.

33. Diggle and Willink attribute these lines to the chorus, but this makes them seem unusually bloodthirsty and emotionally involved: West gives the lines to Electra.

34. Cf. Aesch. *Ag.* 1343-5, *Cho.* 869; Soph. *El.* 1404-16.

35. For fuller discussion of the staging and textual problems here, see Wright, 'Enter a Phrygian'.

36. *Or.* 1490-1 ('Hermione arrived during the falling-to-the-ground murder of her mother ...') is worded in a deliberately ambiguous way – what Willink's commentary (ad loc.) calls 'an ingenious *suggestio falsi*.'

37. See Seidensticker, *Palintonos Harmonia*, pp. 104-6; Porter, *Studies*, pp. 173-213, usefully summarizes and criticizes several variants on this view.

38. Particular caution should be exercised when using Arrowsmith's version in the University of California Press *Collected Greek Tragedies*, Vellacott's Penguin, or West's translation in his otherwise excellent Aris & Phillips commentary.

39. Grüninger, *De Euripidis Oreste*, pp. 11-24, seems to have been the first to make this suggestion (following the suggestion of remarks in the ancient scholia). Porter, *Studies*, pp. 215-50, and Willink in his commentary, pp. 330-1, defend the scene at length.

Notes to pages 47-56

40. Seidensticker, *Palintonos Harmonia* is an excellent study of such light-and-dark effects.
41. Described by Hall and Macintosh, *Greek Tragedy and the British Theatre*, p. 259.
42. The only (partial) parallel for this scene is *Medea* 1317: see Halleran, *Stagecraft*, p. 43.
43. See Davies, 'Speaking and Silence'.
44. On 'closure' in general, see Dunn, *Tragedy's End*.
45. See Chapter 3 below, pp. 69-71.
46. See Walton, *Living Greek Theatre*, p. 369.
47. See Bruce Weber's review of Ellen Beckerman's 2001 production ('What Politicians Those Gods Were', *New York Times*, 6 June 2001).
48. See McDonald, *Living Art of Greek Tragedy*, p. 203.
49. Tricyle Theatre, Kilburn, November 2006: reviewed by A. Wrigley in *Didaskalia* (www.didaskalia.net/reviews/2006/2006_12_21_01.html).

3. Humans and Gods

1. On 'character' and 'characterization' in tragedy, see the various contributions to Pelling (ed.), *Characterization and Individuality*.
2. See West's edition (pp. 59-61) for text and translation of this, the second *hypothesis*. In antiquity this document was attributed to Aristophanes of Byzantium (*c*. 270-190 BC), but all or parts of it may be inauthentic. See Brown, 'Dramatic Synopses'.
3. Porter, *Studies*, pp. 45-6, rightly criticizes those approaches which overemphasize the supposed flaws of Orestes and the others.
4. Verrall, *Essays*, pp. 118-19.
5. See Powell (ed.), *Euripides, Women, and Sexuality* for a variety of interpretations of Euripides' female characters.
6. Conacher, *Euripidean Drama*, p. 217; Mullens, 'The Meaning', pp. 156-8; Verrall, *Essays*, p. 208; Schein, 'Mythical Illusion', pp. 57-8.
7. For such a view see (e.g.) Steiger, *Wie entstand der Orestes?*; Greenberg, 'Euripides' *Orestes:* An Interpretation'.
8. Porter, *Studies*, pp. 45-99.
9. Ronnet, *Sophocle*, pp. 208-9 ('une machine à tuer').
10. See Clarke Kosak, *Heroic Measures*, pp. 131-50: she notes that there is a recurrent focus on concepts of 'therapy' and cure, expressed in language similar to that of texts of the Hippocratic corpus.
11. Hartigan, 'Euripidean Madness'.
12. *Sunesis (xunesis): Orestes* 396; *Heracles* 655-6.
13. See Assael, '*Synesis* dans *Oreste*'; Porter, *Studies*, pp. 20-1 sensibly criticizes anachronistically 'psychological' readings.
14. For example: Democritus (frr. 84, 174, 215, 244, 264 Diels-Kranz); Euripides, *Helen* 1002-3; Sophocles, *Philoctetes* 902-3.

Notes to pages 58-69

15. See discussion on pp. 81-3 below.
16. The issue of the status of those killed in the course of an 'acceptable' act of revenge is, of course, a complex one: see Burnett, *Revenge in Attic and Later Tragedy*.
17. Verrall, *Essays*, p. 211; Burnett, *Catastrophe Survived*, pp. 199-200. Cf. Willink's commentary, p. 94: 'It is important that we should *like* Helen ... that we may be the more shocked by the murderous violence surrounding and directed against her.'
18. Aristotle, *Poetics* 1454a29, 1461b21.
19. West's commentary, pp. 34-5.
20. The text has been questioned here: see Willink's commentary on line 491, which argues that Euripides wrote *agôn tis asophias* (a contest in *un*intelligence).
21. *What* 'laws'? Perhaps the mention of laws is meant to be anachronistic: if so, it may weaken Tyndareus' argument. See Easterling, 'Anachronism', p. 9.
22. So Wolff, *'Orestes'*, p. 351 (referring to Tyndareus' 'fury of vindictiveness'); cf. West's commentary, p. 35 and Kovacs, *Euripides V*, p. 408 on the difficulty of interpreting Tyndareus' character.
23. Verrall, *Essays*, p. 219. Cf. Seidensticker, *Palintonos Harmonia*, pp. 104-6.
24. Whitlock Blundell, *Helping Friends and Harming Enemies*, p. 26.
25. See especially Goldhill, *Reading Greek Tragedy*, pp. 33-56; Seaford, *Reciprocity and Ritual*, pp. 95-7.
26. See Chapter 5 below.
27. For example, Aristophanes, *Women at the Thesmophoria* 450-1; *Frogs* 885-93, 936, etc.
28. Attempts to reconstruct the author's opinions and beliefs from his works alone are now usually seen as doomed to failure (how can we know what Euripides 'really' thought?). See Lefkowitz, ' "Impiety" and "Atheism" in Euripides' for an excellent discussion of the scholarship on this issue.
29. Sourvinou-Inwood, *Tragedy and Athenian Religion*, provides a full and up-to-date discussion of this aspect of tragedy (which is only sketched here).
30. See Willink's commentary ad loc. (cf. *Bacchae* 894, *Heracles* 1263-4, *Helen* 1137). On 'seeming expressions of disbelief' in Euripides, see Stinton, *'Si Credere Dignum Est'*.
31. See West's commentary, p. 222.
32. Strife (*Eris*) is also important in terms of the play's cosmological themes: see Chapter 6 below, pp. 135-6.
33. See, however, Stafford, *Worshipping Virtues*, on post-fifth-century cult worship of *Tychê* and other abstract deities.
34. The ancient *Hypothesis* to the play (attributed, perhaps

wrongly, to Aristophanes of Byzantium) recorded that *Or.* had an ending rather akin to comedy (*komikôteran ... katastrophên*); cf. Dunn, 'Tragic and Comic License'; Knox, 'Euripidean Comedy'.
35. Verrall, *Essays*, pp. 256-7. Verrall was so unhappy with the transmitted ending that he suggested that the play was originally meant to end at line 1624 (before Apollo's epiphany).
36. E.g. Reinhardt, 'Intellectual Crisis', p. 46; Parry, 'Euripides' *Orestes*', p. 338-9; Vellacott, *Ironic Drama*, pp. 78-80, etc.
37. Wolff, '*Orestes*', pp. 355-6.
38. Cf. Euripides, *Helen* 38-41, *Electra* 1281-2 for the same explanation of the war.
39. See Scullion, 'Tradition and Innovation', pp. 220-1; cf. West's commentary, p. 291.
40. For the view that the ending is an example of faulty plot-construction, see (e.g.) di Benedetto, *Euripidis Orestes* on lines 1624-93; cf. Verrall (n. 35 above).

4. Late Euripides

1. *Lineage and Life* 22-3, 34 (Kovacs pp. 6-9); *Souda* E 3695 (Kovacs p. 10); Thomas Magister §11-12 (Kovacs pp. 12-14); cf. Lefkowitz, *Lives of the Greek Poets*, pp. 95-101.
2. Cf. Wilson, *The Outsider* (which controversially discusses artistic originality in the light of modern European existentialism).
3. *Lineage and Life* 4 (Kovacs pp. 2-3); Satyrus fr. 8 II, fr. 39 VII (Kovacs pp. 16-19); Thomas Magister §5 (Kovacs pp. 12-13); [anon.] *On Tragedy* (Kovacs pp. 50-1).
4. For detailed discussion, see Silk and Stern, *Nietzsche on Tragedy*.
5. Nietzsche, *Birth of Tragedy* §10 (tr. Fadiman, p. 36).
6. Schlegel, *Vorlesungen*; Nestle, *Euripides*; see Michelini, *Euripides and the Tragic Tradition* for discussion of some aspects of nineteenth-century Euripidean scholarship.
7. Kranz, *Stasimon*, p. 232 (my translation).
8. Reinhardt, 'Die Sinneskrise bei Euripides' (translated in Mossman, *Euripides*, pp. 16-46).
9. 'The Eternal Fate of the World's Small Individual', *Kathimerini*, Thursday 10 July 2008.
10. Zeitlin, 'Closet of Masks', pp. 51-2, 57-8.
11. Hall, 'Political and Cosmic Turbulence', pp. 284, 277.
12. For balanced (but still doom-laden) accounts of the end of the fifth century, see Hornblower, *The Greek World 479-323 BC*; Hammond, *History of Greece*; *The Cambridge Ancient History* (Cambridge: Cambridge University Press, 2nd edition, 1961-), vol. v. (etc.).
13. These were Euripides' last plays, produced posthumously. It has

Notes to pages 76-86

sometimes been suggested that *Rhesus* (attributed to Euripides) is a fourth-century work by another author: see Ritchie, *Authenticity*.
   14. See Wilson, 'Tragedy in the Fourth Century', in Easterling.
   15. See Wright, *Euripides' Escape-Tragedies* (especially chs 3-5).
   16. For example, West (commentary, pp. 27-8) calls *Or.* simply 'a rattling good play' – pure entertainment, with no deeper meaning at all.
   17. The date of *Or.* is attested by the scholion on line 371. For Euripides' death in 406, see *FGrHist* 239 A 50, 63 (Parian Marble) = *TrGF* 1 DID D a 50, 63.
   18. Said, *On Late Style*, pp. 10-12.
   19. Said, *On Late Style*, p. 27.
   20. Bloom, *The Anxiety of Influence*.
   21. Ar. *Clouds* 534-6 is usually taken as evidence for the revival of the trilogy. See Newiger, 'Elektra in Aristophanes' *Wolken*', and (more sceptically) Bain, '*Electra* 518-44', p. 110.
   22. See Willink's commentary, pp. lv-lvi.
   23. Cf. Willink's commentary, p. lvi, n. 92: 'The points of contact with Sophocles' *Philoctetes* are too numerous to list here ... suffice it to say that, if one reads either play and then immediately the other, one repeatedly experiences a sense of *déjà vu*.'
   24. This similarity is seen as central to the play's meaning by Greenberg, '*Orestes*: An Interpretation', pp. 160-3 ('Helen is a doublet for Clytemnestra').
   25. Zeitlin, 'Closet of Masks', pp. 51-2.
   26. I explore this topic at length elsewhere: Wright, '*Orestes,* A Euripidean Sequel'.
   27. See Wright, *Euripides' Escape-Tragedies*, ch. 4.
   28. Aristophanes, *Women at the Thesmophoria* 849-50. The comic scene and the 'slogan' are discussed by Kannicht in his commentary, vol. 1, p. 21, and Rau, *Paratragodia*, pp. 53-89.
   29. See Chapter 6 below.
   30. See Hall, 'Actor's Song'.
   31. Kovacs, *Euripidea,* pp. 50-1 (but contrast Plut., *Quaest. conv.* 3.1, where the chromatic genus is attributed to Agathon).
   32. On all aspects of 'New Music' see Csapo, 'Later Euripidean Music'; Barker, *Documents,* pp. 93-5; West, *Ancient Greek Music,* pp. 356-72.
   33. The invented word *dyselena* in Greek is hard to translate: it is a compound of *dys-* (ill, unfortunate, wrong) and Helen's name. Cf. *IA* 1316 and the similar 'Dysparis' at Homer, *Iliad* 3.39.
   34. E.g. the intriguing 1999 performances of the Atrium Antiquae Musicae de Madrid, under the direction of Gregorio Paniagua (available on CD on the Harmonia Mundi label: *Musique de la Grèce antique*): this disc includes a recording of *Orestes'* first stasimon.
   35. Pherecrates, fr. 155 (in Kassel and Austin, *Poetae Comici Graeci*).

Notes to pages 86-99

36. Forrest, 'Generation Gap'.
37. Cf. Plato, *Symposium* 215c, *Laws* 669a-670a; Aristotle, *Politics* 1341a, etc. For discussion see Csapo, 'The Politics of the New Music'.
38. D.L. Page (ed.), *Poetae Melici Graeci* (Oxford: Clarendon Press), frr. 796, 798.
39. Satyrus, *Life of Euripides*, fr. 39; cf. Plutarch, *Agesilaus* 14, Pausanias 8.50.
40. Easterling, 'Anachronism'.
41. Verrall, *Essays*, p. 201.

5. Politics

1. See Csapo and Slater, *Context of Ancient Drama*, pp. 103-20; cf. Pickard-Cambridge, *Dramatic Festivals*, pp. 57-101.
2. See Marshall and Van Willigenburg, 'Judging'.
3. Aristotle, *Poetics* 9 1451b5-11.
4. Hall, 'Is There a *Polis* in Aristotle's *Poetics*?'
5. See (e.g.) Allan, 'Euripides in Megale Hellas'; Taplin, *Pots and Plays*, pp. 1-6.
6. See Dobrov (ed.), *The City as Comedy* for a variety of modern approaches to the problem.
7. See Easterling, 'Anachronism.'
8. Goldhill, 'Great Dionysia'. Cf. Goldhill's later article 'Civic Ideology and the Problem of Difference'. Winkler and Zeitlin (ed.), *Nothing to Do with Dionysos?* assembles a collection of broadly similar approaches.
9. Vernant and Vidal-Naquet, *Myth and Tragedy in Ancient Greece*; cf. Segal, *Interpreting Greek Tragedy*.
10. Seaford, *Reciprocity and Ritual*; cf. *Dionysus*.
11. *Reciprocity and Ritual*, p. 344.
12. Croally, *Euripidean Polemic* and 'Tragedy's Teaching'; Gregory, *Euripides and the Instruction of the Athenians*.
13. See especially *Republic* book 10 (with Rowe's commentary).
14. Griffin, 'The Social Function of Attic Tragedy' (Seaford responds in 'The Social Function of Attic Tragedy: a Response to Jasper Griffin'). Cf. Scullion, 'Nothing to Do with Dionysus'.
15. Rhodes, 'Nothing to Do With Democracy'; Carter, 'Was Athenian Tragedy Democratic?'
16. E.g. Aristophanes, *Frogs* 949-52. Excellent discussion of this aspect of tragedy can be found in Hall, 'Sociology'.
17. See any of the authors so far cited; and cf. Goff, *History, Tragedy, Theory*.
18. See, for example, Goldhill, 'Civic Ideology and the Problem of Difference'; Seaford, 'Historicizing Tragic Ambivalence'.
19. Reviewed by Susannah Clapp in the *Observer* (Sunday, 10 April, 2005).

20. Thucydides 1.1, 1.21-4; Herodotus 1.1-5.
21. See Wright, 'Comedy and the Trojan War'.
22. Euripides as 'anti-war' poet: see especially Croally, *Euripidean Polemic*; Vellacott, *Ironic Drama*, pp. 253-77.
23. *Helen* 38-41; in fact this version is first seen in the early Epic Cycle (*Cypria* fr. 1).
24. Euben, 'Political Corruption', p. 231.
25. See W. Allan, *The Andromache and Euripidean Tragedy*, pp. 95-8, 136-44.
26. Fuqua, 'The World of Myth', esp. pp. 11-23: Helen's disappearance is seen as reflecting 'the futility of heroic ideals'.
27. See Thucydides 7.72-87; cf. Macleod, 'Thucydides and Tragedy'.
28. [Aristotle], *Constitution of the Athenians* 29.1. Chs 29-33 of this work deal with the political problems of 411-410. See Rhodes' Penguin edition, pp. 9-35, for an accessible account of the date, authorship and purpose of the work; cf. his larger commentary for fuller discussion.
29. Thucydides 8.96-8; Lysias, *Oration* 20; cf. Andrewes' chapter in *The Cambridge Ancient History* vol. v, pp. 471-81, for a modern account.
30. See Ostwald, *Popular Sovereignty*, pp. 199-218.
31. Hall, 'Political and Cosmic Turbulence', pp. 267-8.
32. Wolff, '*Orestes*', p. 341.
33. Morwood's notes to Waterfield's World's Classics translation, p. 192. Cf. the scholiast on *Orestes* 902ff. (detecting yet another reference to Cleophon).
34. Cf. Greenberg, 'Euripides' *Orestes*'; he sees the contrast between *philia* and *sophia* as central to the play's meaning.
35. Rawson, 'Aspects of *Orestes*', pp. 157-62. Verrall ('Essays', p. 223) had already seen that Orestes and Pylades formed an 'aristocratic treason-club'. Cf. Hall, 'Political and Cosmic Turbulence', pp. 269-71.
36. Translation adapted from Rex Warner's Penguin edition (Harmondsworth: Penguin, 1954).
37. So Willink in his commentary ad loc. (comparing Sophocles, *Ajax* 683 as the only other usage).
38. Hall, 'Political and Cosmic Turbulence', p. 270.
39. West's commentary, p. 265.
40. Porter, *Studies*, pp. 329-31.
41. Rawson, 'Aspects', p. 160; Pelling, *Literary Texts*, p. 188.
42. *Orestes* 46 (*edoxe d'Argei ...*) recalls official formulaic language (see West's commentary ad loc.); *Orestes* 885 (*tis krêzei legein?*) paraphrases *tis agoreuein bouletai?* (attested at Aristophanes, *Acharnians* 45). All the parallels I mention here are noted by Pelling, *Literary Texts*, p. 165.
43. See the commentaries of Willink and West ad loc.
44. Hall, 'Sociology', p. 95.
45. Ibid., p. 125.

46. See Longo, 'The Theater of the *Polis*, pp. 12-19; Vernant and Vidal-Naquet, *Myth and Tragedy* pp. 258, 311-12.
47. Gould, 'Tragedy and Collective Experience'.
48. Wedd's commentary ad loc.
49. (E.g.) Thucydides 3.75.2, 3.81.2, 4.46.4, 4.66.3, 6.35.2; Aristophanes, *Knights* 1128, *Peace* 684. See Ostwald, *From Popular Sovereignty to the Sovereignty of Law*, pp. 199-229.
50. Scholiast on *Or.* 772; cf. scholiast on 903ff. (and West's commentary ad loc.); but Willink in his commentary, p. 206, suspects an interpolation. A similar sentiment and phrasing (Gk. *prostatai* again) are seen at Eur., *Suppliant Women* 243.
51. West, for example, deletes 906-13, 916, 933; Willink deletes an even greater proportion (904-13, 916, 932-42). See their respective commentaries for discussion.
52. See Allan (ed.), *Children of Heracles*, pp. 43-6, and the Introduction to Morwood (ed.), *Suppliant Women*.
53. On ideological opposition to democracy in fifth-century writings, see Ostwald, *Popular Sovereignty*, and the Introduction to Marr and Rhodes (ed.), *Old Oligarch*.
54. On Apollo's epiphany, see Chapter 3 above.

6. Euripides' Cleverest Play

1. See Kassel and Austin, *Poetae Comici Graeci*, vol. vii.
2. See Rau, *Paratragodia*, pp. 53-89; cf. Bowie, *Aristophanes*, pp. 217-27.
3. See the Introduction to Dover's edition of *Frogs*, pp. 10-24; cf. Dover's edition of *Clouds*, pp. 106-13.
4. E.g. *Clouds* 547-8.
5. E.g. Aristophanes, *Clouds* 1369-70, 1378; *Women at the Thesmophoria* 21; *Lysistrata* 368.
6. Aristophanes, *Clouds* 148, 331, 418 (etc.); Phrynichus, *Muses* fr. 32.
7. 'Philosopher of the stage': Vitruvius, *On Architecture* 8 pr. 1; Athenaeus 4.48, 158e (etc.). On the biographers' treatment of Euripides' relationship with philosophers, see Kovacs, *Euripidea*, pp. 1-27, and the Introduction to Kovacs' Loeb edition: *Euripides I*, pp. 1-35.
8. For English translations of the sophists' work, with good discussion, see Dillon and Gergel (ed.), *The Greek Sophists*; cf. Kerferd, *The Sophistic Movement*.
9. However, Socrates did blame Aristophanic comedy, in part, for the Athenians' hostility to him in 399 BC: *Apology* 19c.
10. For other modern views of Euripides' supposed lack of depth, see

Burnett, 'A Comedy of Ideas', Knox, 'Euripidean Comedy', and the commentaries of West and Willink.
11. Winnington-Ingram, 'Euripides: *poiêtês sophos*', pp. 127-38.
12. Nietzsche, *Birth of Tragedy*, §§12, 76. See Wright, *Escape-Tragedies*, pp. 242-5 for discussion.
13. See Wright, *Escape-Tragedies*, pp. 228-337.
14. The term 'metatheatre' was invented in relation to modern theatre, but see Dobrov, *Figures of Play* for its application to ancient Greek drama.
15. E.g. Taplin, 'A *Synkrisis*'.
16. For two contrasting views on 'metatheatricality' and related effects, see Dobrov, *Figures of Play* and Rosenmeyer, 'Metatheater: An Essay on Overload'.
17. *Concise Oxford English Dictionary*, s.v. 'Irony' (3).
18. West, *Commentary*, p. 197, quoting Heraclitus fr. 56 Markovich (DK22 B84).
19. See Cropp's edition of *Electra*, pp. 134-40. Most recent discussion of the *Electra* scene (with bibliography) can be found in Davies, 'Euripides' *Electra*: The Recognition Scene Again'.
20. Scholiast on *Orestes* 1421; see Willink's commentary ad loc. for textual discussion.
21. See Collard, Cropp and Gibert, *Selected Fragmentary Plays II*, for full discussion of the fragments of *Andromeda*.
22. Winnington-Ingram, 'Euripides: *poiêtês sophos*', p. 52.
23. Davies, 'Speaking and Silence'.
24. E.g. Zeitlin, 'Closet of Masks'.
25. See Taplin, 'A *Synkrisis*'.
26. Cf. Chapter 4 above (on the 'New Musical' revolution).
27. Timotheus, fr. 796; Aristophanes, *Wasps* 1016-50, *Women at the Thesmophoria* 849-50.
28. West's commentary, p. 251.
29. Restrictions of space compel me to oversimplify this huge and complex topic. For more discussion see (e.g.) Csapo, *Theories of Mythology* or (for a very different approach) Veyne, *Did the Greeks Believe in their Myths?*
30. Dillon and Gergel (ed.), *The Greek Sophists*, pp. 66-76.
31. Gomperz, *Sophistik und Rhetorik*, p. 35 ('philosophische Nihilismus').
32. See Wright, *Escape-Tragedies*, pp. 260-337.
33. Cf. *Orestes* 126, 252, 314-15, 331, 407, 640-1, 669, 819, 1118, 1204-5, 1298, 1556-60.
34. There is a textual problem here. With West, I adopt Paley's emendation (*tode dokein*) rather than the manuscript reading (*tôide Dokein*), which if correct would mean that Pylades is telling Orestes to

Notes to pages 131-136

'pray to Illusion' (as if *Dokein*, 'Illusion', were a deity). But this is unnatural in Greek: see West's commentary, p. 236 for discussion.
35. Cf. pp. 63-4 above.
36. These and other rhetorical tropes are fully discussed in Michael Lloyd's superb book, *The Agon in Euripides*, pp. 19-36.
37. See pp. 58-9.
38. Or, alternatively, 'an *agôn* of *stupidity*' (if Willink's conjecture *agôn tis asophias* is correct). See Willink's commentary ad loc.
39. Diels and Kranz, *Fragmente der Vorsokratiker*, 59 A 42 (cf. B9, B13). Translation taken from Waterfield, *The First Philosophers*, p. 128.
40. See West's commentary ad loc.; cf. Aristophanes, *Clouds* 380 with Dover's commentary.
41. See Scodel, 'Tantalus and Anaxagoras'; cf. West's commentary, p. 252. Homer, *Iliad* 8.19-27 may be a relevant source.
42. Diels and Kranz, *Fragmente der Vorsokratiker*, 22 B80, B53; 31 B20. See Hall, 'Political and Cosmic Turbulence', pp. 271-2.
43. See pp. 103-6 above.
44. Hall, 'Political and Cosmic Turbulence', p. 280.

Guide to Further Reading

The notes to each chapter consist largely of references to works which are relevant to specific points in the main text. What follows here is a general bibliographical guide which aims to help the reader navigate the huge sea of secondary literature relating to *Orestes* and Greek drama.

Editions and commentaries

The standard modern edition of *Orestes* (which I have used while writing this book) is James Diggle's Oxford Classical Text (*Euripidis Fabulae* iii, Oxford: Oxford University Press, 1993): it is equipped with an extremely detailed and reliable *apparatus criticus*. For further discussion of the text's history and the readings which Diggle adopts, see his earlier study *The Textual Tradition of Euripides' Orestes* (Oxford: Clarendon Press, 1991) and the Index Locorum in his *Euripidea* (Oxford: Clarendon Press, 1994). On the survival and transmission of tragic texts in general, Robert Garland's *Surviving Greek Tragedy* (London: Duckworth, 2004) is an entertaining guide for the non-specialist reader.

David Kovacs' complete edition of Euripides in the Loeb Classical Texts series (Cambridge, MA: Loeb, 1990-2002) provides another good modern text and apparatus, though his judgements often differ from Diggle's. See Kovacs' *Euripidea Tertia* (Leiden: Brill, 2003) for full discussion of the text which he prints.

We are fortunate to possess two excellent critical commentaries in English. Charles Willink's commentary (Oxford: Clarendon Press, 1986) is the more substantial of the two: it contains a wealth of textual, metrical, philological and interpretative material. Willink reprints the older (now obsolete) Oxford Classical Text of Gilbert Murray, but at numerous points he suggests different readings. West's edition in the Aris & Phillips series (Warminster 1987), aimed at a slightly less advanced reader, is similarly packed with judicious and useful material: it also contains a parallel English translation (though this tends to give the impression that the play is much funnier than it really is).

Euripides: Orestes

Both Willink and West were granted pre-publication access to the new OCT, so that their commentaries can conveniently be used alongside Diggle's text. In Italian, there is also V. di Benedetto's commentary (Firenze: La nuova Italia, 1965).

Translations

A large number of English versions exist: deciding which of them is 'the best' will inevitably be a matter of personal taste. My own preferred translations, written in prose which is clear, unpretentious and faithful to the Greek sentence structure, are those of Kovacs in his Loeb volume (see above) and James Waterfield in his World's Classics edition (which contains an introduction by Edith Hall and notes by James Morwood: *Orestes and Other Plays*, Oxford: Oxford University Press, 2001). The popular verse translation by William Arrowsmith in the University of Chicago *Complete Greek Tragedies* (Chicago 1958) probably works better as a version for actors, though it is less close to the Greek (especially in the choral passages and the difficult aria of the Phrygian slave). I am not a fan of the Penguin Classics edition by Philip Vellacott (*Orestes and Other Plays*, Harmondsworth: Penguin, 1972): this is also a widely used verse translation, designed for acting purposes, but it often transforms Euripides' Greek into jaunty, quasi-comical or even banal English. Similarly, I would be inclined to avoid the older Loeb edition by A.S. Way (Cambridge, MA: Loeb, 1912), which now seems fussily quaint and archaic.

Greek tragedy: general

Again, a large number of introductory books exist: my selection of a few of these works merely reflects personal preference. The new *Companion to Greek Tragedy*, edited by Justina Gregory (Oxford: Blackwell 2005) is a superb collection of essays by many of the leading specialists in the subject, as is Pat Easterling's *Cambridge Companion to Greek Tragedy* (Cambridge: Cambridge University Press, 1997). Edith Hall's recent book *The Theatrical Cast of Athens* (Oxford: Oxford University Press, 2006) is a stimulating and highly readable account of the interactions between Athenian drama and everyday life: she manages to recreate a real sense of what it was like to be a fifth-century Athenian and to attend the dramatic festivals. Eric Csapo and William Slater's source-book, *The Context of Ancient Drama* (Ann Arbor: University of Michigan Press, 1994), presents (in English translation) much of the ancient evidence for our knowledge of the classical theatre.

Guide to Further Reading

Euripides: general

Christopher Collard's pamphlet *Euripides* (Oxford: Greece and Rome New Surveys in the Classics, 1981) provides an admirably large amount of introductory material in a short space. The definitive modern book on Euripides has yet to be written. In the meantime we have T.B.L. Webster's *Tragedies of Euripides* (London: Methuen, 1967), the only book to discuss Euripides' entire life and work together (including the lost plays): it is starting to show its age, but is still a wonderfully readable and scholarly account of the plays themselves. Judith Mossman's *Oxford Readings in Euripides* (Oxford: Oxford University Press, 2003) is a book of well-chosen essays which collectively give a sense of Euripides and his place in modern scholarship: her Introduction in particular (pp. 1-15) is well worth reading.

Orestes: general

Apart from the commentaries mentioned above, John Porter's *Studies in Euripides' Orestes* (Leiden: Brill, 1994) is the essential reference work: it deals not only with *Orestes* itself but also with nearly all previous scholarly interpretations of *Orestes*. Porter's critique of the scholarly tradition, and his own reading of the play, is always highly judicious. A more provocative introduction to the play is provided by A.W. Verrall, that much-maligned Cambridge don, who wrote a superb chapter on *Orestes* in his *Essays on Four Plays of Euripides* (Cambridge: Cambridge University Press, 1905): like most of his work, it contains much that is wayward and bizarre, but it is also highly perceptive and entertaining. Not dissimilar to Verrall, though much less eccentric, is Christian Wolff's powerful essay, '*Orestes*', in E. Segal (ed.), *Euripides: A Collection of Critical Essays* (Englewood Hills: Prentice-Hall, 1968), pp. 132-49; reprinted in E. Segal (ed.), *Oxford Readings in Greek Tragedy* (Oxford: Oxford University Press, 1983), pp. 340-56. Another provocative, but more recent, treatment of the play is Froma Zeitlin's article 'The Closet of Masks: Role-Playing and Myth-Making in the *Orestes* of Euripides', *Ramus* 9 (1980), pp. 51-77; reprinted in Mossman's *Readings* (see above), pp. 309-41.

Stagecraft

Oliver Taplin's classic book *Greek Tragedy in Action* (London: Methuen, 1978), which can be seen as having sparked off the 'theatrical revolution' in classical studies, is still essential reading. More recent studies include David Wiles' *Tragedy in Athens: Performance Space and Theatrical Meaning* (Cambridge: Cambridge University Press, 1997) and *Greek Theatre Performance* (Cambridge: Cambridge

Euripides: Orestes

University Press, 2000), Michael Halleran's brief but useful book *Stagecraft in Euripides* (London: Croom Helm, 1985), and Clifford Ashby's sensibly sceptical study *Classical Greek Theatre: New Views of An Old Subject* (Iowa City: University of Iowa Press, 1998). The last of these books is lavishly illustrated with superb photographs and line drawings.

Novelty, incongruity and 'late Euripides'

W.G Arnott's article 'Euripides and the Unexpected', *Greece and Rome* 20 (1973), pp. 49-63, is a good short study of Euripides' theatrical technique and *penchant* for creating surprise. A.N. Michelini's book *Euripides and the Tragic Tradition* (Madison: University of Wisconsin Press, 1987) argues that Euripidean tragedy is recurrently characterized by its rejection of the normal tragic conventions. On the 'New Music' in particular, see A. Barker, *Greek Musical Writings*, vol. 1 (Cambridge: Cambridge University Press, 1984), pp. 93-116; M.L. West, *Ancient Greek Music* (Oxford: Clarendon Press, 1992), pp. 356-72; and E. Csapo, 'The Politics of the New Music', in P. Murray and P. Wilson (eds.), *Music and the Muses* (Oxford: Oxford University Press, 2004), pp. 207-48.

An influential treatment of 'late Euripides' is given by Karl Reinhardt's essay 'Die Sinneskrise bei Euripides', *Eranos* 26 (1957), pp. 279-317: this is usefully provided in an English translation, 'The Intellectual Crisis in Euripides', in Mossman's *Readings* (see above), pp. 16-46. A different view of 'late Euripides' which relates specifically to *Orestes*, and which tries to account for the precise nature of the play's 'self-conscious' tone, is my own article '*Orestes*, a Euripidean Sequel', *Classical Quarterly* 56 (2006), pp. 33-48.

Philosophy and intellectualism

Reinhardt's essay 'Die Sinneskrise' (see above) creates a well-known image of Euripides *qua* intellectual. Also reprinted in Mossman's collection (pp. 47-63) is R.P. Winnington-Ingram's frequently cited article 'Euripides: *Poiêtês Sophos*', *Arethusa* 2 (1969), pp. 127-42. Winnington-Ingram tends to downplay Euripides' philosophy; a similar tendency is seen in D.J. Conacher's book *Euripides and the Sophists* (London: Duckworth, 1998), though both of these studies repay careful reading. In my own book *Euripides' Escape-Tragedies* (Oxford: Oxford University Press, 2005) I deal with Euripidean drama in relation to the Greek philosophical tradition, arguing that Euripides can be seen as a serious thinker and not 'merely' a dramatist. On philosophical echoes in *Orestes* in particular, see E.M. Hall's brilliant article 'Political and Cosmic Turbulence in Euripides' *Orestes*', in A.H.

Guide to Further Reading

Sommerstein et al. (eds), *Tragedy, Comedy and the Polis* (Bari: Levante, 1993), pp. 263-85.

Fifth-century history, politics and rhetoric

For a balanced narrative history of Athens in and around 408, see D.M. Lewis et al. (eds), *The Cambridge Ancient History*, vol. 5 (2nd edition, Cambridge: Cambridge University Press, 1992), esp. pp. 268-86, 464-98. On the civic and religious aspects of tragedy in general, see J. Winkler and F. Zeitlin (eds), *Nothing to Do With Dionysos? Athenian Drama in its Social Context* (Princeton: Princeton University Press, 1990). Hall's article 'Political and Cosmic Turbulence' (see above) links contemporary politics to the plot of *Orestes*. C.B.R. Pelling, *Literary Texts and the Greek Historian* (London: Routledge, 2000), pp. 164-88 ('Tragedy and Ideology') discusses the ways in which tragedy may be seen as exploring contemporary political and ideological issues. On rhetoric and the *agôn*, see M. Lloyd, *The Agôn in Euripides* (Oxford: Clarendon Press, 1992).

Characterization

Christopher Gill's *Personality in Greek Epic, Tragedy and Philosophy* (Oxford: Clarendon Press, 1996) provides a comprehensive and highly nuanced study of the issues. Shorter but extremely useful discussions of dramatic character include J. Gould, 'Dramatic Character and "Human Intelligibility" in Greek Tragedy', *Proceedings of the Cambridge Philological Society* 24 (1978), 43-67, and P.E. Easterling, 'Constructing Character in Greek Tragedy', in C.B.R. Pelling (ed.), *Characterization and Individuality in Greek Literature* (Oxford: Clarendon Press, 1990), pp. 83-99.

Religion and ritual

Walter Burkert's *Greek Religion* (Oxford 1985) is a very good general introduction to the subject, while Christiane Sourvinou-Inwood's *Tragedy and Athenian Religion* (Lexington, MD: Lexington Books, 2003) deals with the specific question of the relationship between tragedy and real-life religious practice. Her earlier essay 'Tragedy and Religion: Constructs and Meanings', in C.B.R. Pelling (ed.), *Greek Tragedy and the Historian* (Oxford: Clarendon Press, 1997), pp. 161-86, states her main approach in what may be a more digestible format. J.D. Mikalson's *Honor Thy Gods: Popular Religion in Greek Tragedy* (Chapel Hill, NC: University of California Press, 1991) represents a completely different approach to the problem of 'tragic' *versus* 'real' religion. Richard Seaford's marvellous book *Reciprocity and Ritual:*

Euripides: Orestes

Homer and Tragedy in the Developing City-State (Oxford: Clarendon Press, 1994) is a highly idiosyncratic study of the connection between drama and ritual. On the specific question of '*deus ex machina*' endings, see F. Dunn, *Tragedy's End: Closure and Innovation in Euripidean Drama* (Oxford and New York: Oxford University Press, 1996).

Bibliography

The bibliography lists the works cited in the text and notes.

M. Alexiou, *The Ritual Lament in Greek Tradition* (Cambridge: Cambridge University Press, 1974).
W. Allan, *The* Andromache *and Euripidean Tragedy* (Oxford: Oxford University Press, 2000).
—— 'Euripides in Megale Hellas: Some Aspects of the Early Reception of Tragedy', *Greece and Rome* 48 (2001), pp. 67-88.
C. Ashby, *Classical Greek Theatre* (Iowa City: University of Iowa Press, 1999).
J. Assael, '*Synesis* dans *Oreste* d'Euripide', *Acta Classica* 65 (1996), pp. 53-69.
D.M. Bain, *Actors and Audience: A Study of Asides and Related Conventions in Greek Drama* (Oxford: Clarendon Press, 1977).
—— '*Electra* 518-44', *Bulletin of the Institute of Classical Studies* 24 (1977), pp. 104-16.
A. Barker, *Documents of Ancient Greek Music* (Cambridge: Cambridge University Press, 1984).
W.N. Bates, *Euripides, A Student of Human Nature*, 2nd edition (Pennsylvania: University of Pennsylvania Press, 1961).
V. di Benedetto (ed.), *Euripidis Orestes* (Florence: La nuova Italia, 1965).
H. Bloom, *The Anxiety of Influence* (New York: Oxford University Press, 1973).
A.M. Bowie, 'The Parabasis in Aristophanes: Prolegomena: *Acharnians*', *Classical Quarterly* 32 (1982), pp. 27-40.
A.L. Brown, 'The Dramatic Synopses attributed to Aristophanes of Byzantium', *Classical Quarterly* 37 (1987), pp. 427-31.
P. Burian, 'Myth into *Mythos:* The Shaping of Tragic Plot', in P.E. Easterling (ed.), *The Cambridge Companion to Greek Tragedy* (Cambridge: Cambridge University Press, 1997), pp. 178-208.
A.P. Burnett, *Catastrophe Survived: Euripides' Plays of Mixed Reversal* (Oxford: Clarendon Press, 1971).

―――― 'Euripides' *Helen:* A Comedy of Ideas', *Classical Philology* 55 (1960), pp. 151-63 (as 'A. Pippin').
―――― *Revenge in Attic and Later Tragedy* (Oxford and New York: Oxford University Press, 1998).
D. Carter, 'Was Athenian Tragedy Democratic?', *Polis* 21 (2004), pp. 1-25.
J. Clarke Kosak, *Heroic Measures: Hippocratic Medicine in the Making of Euripidean Tragedy* (Leiden: Brill, 2004).
C. Collard, M.J. Cropp and J. Gibert (eds), *Euripides: Selected Fragmentary Plays II* (Oxford: Aris & Phillips, 2004).
D.J. Conacher, *Euripidean Drama* (Toronto: University of Toronto Press, 1961).
―――― *Euripides and the Sophists* (London: Duckworth, 1998).
―――― 'Rhetoric and Relevance in Euripidean Drama', *American Journal of Philology* 102 (1981), pp. 3-25.
N. Croally, *Euripidean Polemic* (Cambridge: Cambridge University Press, 1994).
―――― 'Tragedy's Teaching', in J. Gregory (ed.), *A Companion to Greek Tragedy* (Oxford: Blackwell, 2005), pp. 55-70.
E. Csapo, 'Later Euripidean Music', *Illinois Classical Studies* 24-5 (1999-2000), pp. 399-426.
―――― 'The Politics of the New Music', in P. Wilson and P. Murray (eds), *Music and the Muses: The Culture of Mousike in the Classical Athenian City* (Oxford: Oxford University Press, 2004), pp. 207-48.
―――― *Theories of Mythology* (Oxford: Blackwell, 2005).
E. Csapo and W. Slater, *The Context of Ancient Drama* (Ann Arbor: University of Michigan Press, 1994).
J. Davidson, 'Theatrical Production', in J. Gregory (ed.), *A Companion to Greek Tragedy* (Oxford: Blackwell, 2005), pp. 194-211.
M. Davies, *The Epic Cycle* (Bristol: Bristol Classical Press, 1989).
―――― 'Euripides' *Electra:* The Recognition Scene Again', *Classical Quarterly* 48 (1998), pp. 389-403.
―――― 'Speaking and Silence (Euripides, *Orestes* 1591-2)', *Prometheus* 25 (1999), pp. 227-30.
H. Diels and W. Kranz, *Die Fragmente der Vorsokratiker* (6th edition, Berlin: Weidmann, 1952).
J. Diggle, *The Textual Tradition of Euripides' Orestes* (Oxford: Clarendon Press, 1991).
J. Dillon and T. Gergel (ed.), *The Greek Sophists* (London: Penguin, 2003).
G. Dobrov (ed.), *The City as Comedy* (Iowa City: Iowa University Press, 1997).
―――― *Figures of Play: Greek Drama and Metafictional Poetics* (New York: Oxford University Press, 2001).
K. Dover (ed.), *Aristophanes: Clouds* (Oxford: Clarendon Press, 1968).

Bibliography

────── (ed.), *Aristophanes: Frogs* (Oxford: Clarendon Press, 1993).
J. Duchemin, *L'agôn dans la tragédie grecque* (Paris: Les Belles Lettres, 1945).
F.M. Dunn, 'Tragic and Comic License in Euripides' *Orestes*', *Classical Antiquity* 8 (1989), pp. 238-51.
────── *Tragedy's End: Closure and Innovation in Euripidean Drama* (New York: Oxford University Press, 1996).
P.E. Easterling, 'Anachronism in Greek Tragedy', *Journal of Hellenic Studies* 105 (1985), pp. 1-10.
──────(ed.), *The Cambridge Companion to Greek Tragedy* (Cambridge: Cambridge University Press, 1997).
H. Erbse, *Studien zum Prolog der euripideischen Tragödie* (Berlin: de Gruyter, 1984).
P. Euben, 'Political Corruption in Euripides' *Orestes*', in *Greek Tragedy and Political Theory* (Berkeley and Los Angeles: University of California Press, 1986), pp. 222-51.
W.G. Forrest, 'An Athenian Generation Gap', *Yale Classical Studies* 24 (1975), pp. 37-52.
C. Fuqua, 'The World of Myth in Euripides' *Orestes*', *Traditio* 32 (1976), pp. 1-28.
B. Goff, *History, Tragedy, Theory: Dialogues on Athenian Drama* (Austin: University of Texas Press, 1995).
S. Goldhill, *Reading Greek Tragedy* (Cambridge: Cambridge University Press, 1986).
────── 'The Great Dionysia and Civic Ideology', *Journal of Hellenic Studies* 107 (1987), pp. 58-76.
────── 'Civic Ideology and the Problem of Difference: The Politics of Aeschylean Tragedy, Once Again', *Journal of Hellenic Studies* 120 (2000), pp. 34-56.
H. Gomperz, *Sophistik und Rhetorik* (Leipzig: Teubner, 1912).
J. Gould, 'Tragedy and Collective Experience', in M.S. Silk (ed.), *Tragedy and the Tragic: Greek Theatre and Beyond* (Oxford: Clarendon Press, 1996), pp. 217-43.
B. Goward, *Telling Tragedy: Narrative Technique in Aeschylus, Sophocles and Euripides* (London: Duckworth, 1999).
N. Greenberg, 'Euripides' *Orestes:* An Interpretation', *Harvard Studies in Classical Philology* 66 (1962), pp. 157-92.
J. Gregory, *Euripides and the Instruction of the Athenians* (Ann Arbor: University of Michigan Press, 1991).
J. Griffin, 'The Social Function of Attic Tragedy', *Classical Quarterly* 48 (1998), pp. 39-61.
G. Grube, *The Drama of Euripides* (London: Methuen, 1941).
A. Grüninger, *De Euripidis Oreste* (Basle: Birhaüser, 1898).
E.M. Hall, 'Actor's Song in Greek Tragedy', in S. Goldhill and R.

Euripides: Orestes

Osborne (eds), *Performance Culture and Athenian Democracy* (Cambridge: Cambridge University Press, 1999), pp. 96-122.

——— 'Is there a Polis in Aristotle's *Poetics*?' in M. Silk (ed.), *Tragedy and the Tragic: Greek Theatre and Beyond* (Oxford: Clarendon Press, 1996), pp. 295-309.

——— 'Political and Cosmic Turbulence in Euripides' *Orestes*', in A.H. Sommerstein et al. (eds), *Tragedy, Comedy and the Polis* (Bari: Levante, 1993), pp. 263-85.

——— 'The Sociology of Athenian Tragedy', in P.E. Easterling (ed.), *The Cambridge Companion to Greek Tragedy* (Cambridge: Cambridge University Press, 1997), pp. 93-126.

E.M. Hall and F. Macintosh, *Greek Tragedy on the British Stage* (Oxford: Oxford University Press, 2005).

M. Halleran, *The Stagecraft of Euripides* (London: Croom Helm, 1985).

S.J. Halliwell, *Aristotle's* Poetics (London: Duckworth, 1986).

E. Handley and R. Green, *Images of the Greek Theatre* (London: British Museum Press, 1995).

K. Hartigan, 'Euripidean Madness: Herakles and Orestes', *Greece and Rome* 34 (1987), pp. 126-35.

——— *Greek Tragedy on the American Stage* (Westport, CT: Greenwood Press, 1995).

M. Heath, *The Poetics of Greek Tragedy* (London: Duckworth, 1987).

S. Hornblower, *The Greek World 479-323 BC* (London: Routledge, 1983).

R. Kannicht, *Euripides: Helena* (Heidelberg: Winter, 1969).

——— *Tragicorum Graecorum Fragmenta*, vol. 5: *Euripides* (Göttingen: Vandenheock und Ruprecht, 2004).

R. Kassel and C. Austin, *Poetae Comici Graeci* (Berlin: de Gruyter, 1983-).

G. Kerferd, *The Sophistic Movement* (Cambridge: Cambridge University Press, 1981).

H.D.F. Kitto, *Greek Tragedy*, 3rd edition (London: Methuen, 1961).

B.M.W. Knox, 'Euripidean Comedy', in *Word and Action: Essays on the Ancient Theater* (Baltimore: John Hopkins, 1979), pp. 250-74.

D. Kovacs, *Euripidea* (Leiden: Brill, 1994).

——— *Euripides V* (Cambridge, MA: Loeb, 2002).

W. Kranz, *Stasimon* (Berlin: Weidmann, 1933).

M. Lefkowitz, ' "Impiety" and "Atheism" in Euripidean Drama', *Classical Quarterly* 39 (1989), pp. 70-82.

——— *The Lives of the Greek Poets* (London: Duckworth, 1981).

M. Lloyd, *The Agon in Euripides* (Oxford: Clarendon Press, 1992).

O. Longo, 'The Theater of the *Polis*', in J. Winkler and F. Zeitlin (eds), *Nothing to do with Dionysos?* (New Jersey: Princeton University Press, 1990), pp. 12-19.

F. Lucas, *Tragedy*, 2nd edition (London: Hogarth Press, 1957).

Bibliography

C.W. Macleod, 'Thucydides and Tragedy', in *Collected Essays* (Oxford: Clarendon Press, 1983), pp. 140-58.
M. McDonald, *The Living Art of Greek Tragedy* (Bloomington: Indiana University Press, 2003).
J. Marr and P.J. Rhodes (eds), *The Old Oligarch: Constitution of the Athenians* (Oxford: Aris & Phillips, 2008).
C.W. Marshall and S. Van Willigenburg, 'Judging Athenian Dramatic Competitions', *Journal of Hellenic Studies* 124 (2004), pp. 90-107.
A.N. Michelini, *Euripides and the Tragic Tradition* (Madison: University of Wisconsin Press, 1987).
J. Morwood (ed.), *Euripides: Suppliant Women* (Oxford: Aris & Phillips, 2006).
H.G. Mullens, 'The Meaning of Euripides' *Orestes*', *Classical Quarterly* 34 (1940), pp. 153-8.
W. Nestle, *Euripides, der Dichter der griechischen Aufklärung* (2nd edition, Aalen: Scientia Verlag, 1969).
H.J. Newiger, 'Elektra in Aristophanes' *Wolken*', *Hermes* 89 (1961), pp. 422-30.
F. Nietzsche, *The Birth of Tragedy*, tr. C.P. Fadiman (New York: Dover, 1995). [Originally published as *Die Geburt der Tragödie, oder Griechenthum und Pessimismus*, Leipzig, 1872.]
M. Ostwald, *From Popular Sovereignty to the Sovereignty of Law* (Berkeley: University of California Press, 1986).
D.L. Page, *Actors' Interpolations in Greek Tragedy* (Oxford: Oxford University Press, 1934).
H. Parry, 'Euripides' *Orestes*: The Quest for Salvation', *Transactions and Proceedings of the American Philological Association* 100 (1969), pp. 337-53.
H. Patin, *Études sur les tragiques grecs: Euripide* (Paris: Hachette, 1893).
C.B.R. Pelling (ed.), *Characterization and Individuality in Greek Literature* (Oxford: Clarendon Press, 1990).
―― *Literary Texts and the Greek Historian* (London: Routledge, 2000).
A.W. Pickard-Cambridge, *The Dramatic Festivals of Athens*, 2nd edition, rev. D.M. Lewis and J. Gould (Oxford: Clarendon Press, 1988).
E. Pöhlmann and M.L. West, *Documents of Ancient Greek Music* (Oxford: Oxford University Press, 2001).
J. Porter, *Studies in Euripides' Orestes* (Leiden: Brill, 1994).
A. Powell (ed.), *Euripides, Women and Sexuality* (London: Routledge, 1990).
P. Rau, *Paratragodia* (Munich: Beck, 1967).
E. Rawson, 'Aspects of Euripides' *Orestes*', *Arethusa* 5 (1972), pp. 155-67.
K. Reinhardt, 'The Intellectual Crisis in Euripides', in J. Mossman

Euripides: Orestes

(ed.), *Oxford Readings in Euripides* (Oxford: Oxford University Press, 2003), pp. 16-46 [originally published in as 'Die Sinneskrise bei Euripides', *Eranos* 26 (1957), pp. 279-317].
W. Ritchie, *The Authenticity of the Rhesus of Euripides* (Cambridge: Cambridge University Press, 1964).
P.J. Rhodes, 'Nothing to Do with Democracy: Athenian Drama and the Polis', *Journal of Hellenic Studies* 123 (2003), pp. 104-19.
G. Ronnet, *Sophocle: poète tragique* (Paris: de Boccard, 1969).
T.J. Rosenmeyer, 'Metatheater: An Essay on Overload', *Arion* 10 (2002), pp. 97-119.
C.J. Rowe (ed.), *Plato: Republic 10* (Warminster: Aris & Phillips, 1993).
E. Said, *On Late Style* (London: Bloomsbury, 2006).
S.L. Schein, 'Mythical Illusion and Historical Reality in Euripides' Orestes', *Wiener Studien* 9 (1975), pp. 49-66.
A. Schlegel, *Vorlesungen über dramatische Kunst und Literatur* (Bonn and Leipzig: Schroeder, 1923).
R. Scodel, 'Tantalus and Anaxagoras', *Harvard Studies in Classical Philology* 88 (1984), pp. 13-24.
S. Scullion, 'Nothing to do with Dionysus: Tragedy Misconceived as Ritual', *Classical Quarterly* 52 (2002), pp. 102-37.
—— 'Tradition and Innovation in Euripidean Aitiology', *Illinois Classical Studies* 24-5 (1999-2000), pp. 217-33.
R.A.S. Seaford, *Reciprocity and Ritual: Homer and Tragedy in the Developing City-State* (Oxford: Clarendon Press, 1994).
—— 'Historicizing Tragic Ambivalence: The Vote of Athena', in B. Goff (ed.), *History, Tragedy, Theory* (Austin: University of Texas Press, 1995).
—— 'The Social Function of Attic Tragedy: A Response to Jasper Griffin', *Classical Quarterly* 50 (2000), pp. 30-44.
—— *Dionysos* (London: Routledge, 2006).
C.P. Segal, *Interpreting Greek Tragedy* (Ithaca, NY: Cornell University Press, 1986).
B. Seidensticker, *Palintonos Harmonia: Studien zu komischen Elementen in der griechischen Tragödie* (Göttingen: Vandenhoeck und Ruprecht, 1982).
M. Silk and J. Stern, *Nietzsche on Tragedy* (Cambridge: Cambridge University Press, 1981).
F. Solmsen, 'Euripides Ion im Vergleich mit anderen Tragödien', *Hermes* 69 (1934), pp. 391-408.
C. Sourvinou-Inwood, *Tragedy and Athenian Religion* (Lanham, MD: Lexington, 2003).
A. Spira, *Untersuchungen zum Deus ex Machina bei Sophokles und Euripides* (Kallmunz: Lassleben, 1960).

Bibliography

E. Stafford, *Worshipping Virtues* (London and Swansea: Duckworth and Classical Press of Wales, 1999).
H. Steiger, 'Wie entstand der Orestes der Euripides?', *Philologus* 67 (1908), pp. 202-37.
T.C.W. Stinton, '*Si credere dignum est:* Some Expressions of Disbelief in Euripides and Others', *Proceedings of the Cambridge Philological Society* 202 (1976), pp. 60-89.
O.P. Taplin, *Greek Tragedy in Action* (London: Methuen, 1978).
——— 'Fifth-Century Tragedy and Comedy: A *Synkrisis*', *Journal of Hellenic Studies* 106 (1986), pp. 163-174.
——— *Pots and Plays* (New York: Getty, 2007).
P. Vellacott, *Ironic Drama: A Study of Euripides' Method and Meaning* (Cambridge: Cambridge University Press, 1975).
J.P. Vernant and P. Vidal-Naquet, *Myth and Tragedy in Ancient Greece* (New York: Oxford University Press, translated by J. Lloyd, 1990).
A.W. Verrall, *Essays on Four Plays of Euripides* (Cambridge: Cambridge University Press, 1905).
P. Veyne, *Did the Greeks Believe in their Myths?* (translated by J. Lloyd, Chicago: University of Chicago Press, 1988).
J.M. Walton, *The Living Greek Theatre: A Handbook of Classical Performance and Modern Production* (New York: Greenwood Press, 1987).
R. Waterfield (ed.), *The First Philosophers: The Presocratics and Sophists* (Oxford: Oxford University Press, 2000).
N. Wedd (ed.), *Euripides: Orestes* (Cambridge: Cambridge University Press, 1895).
M.L. West (ed.), *Euripides: Orestes* (Warminster: Aris & Phillips, 1987).
M. Whitlock Blundell, *Helping Friends and Harming Enemies: A Study of Sophocles and Greek Ethics* (Cambridge: Cambridge University Press, 1989).
D. Wiles, *Greek Theatre Production* (Cambridge: Cambridge University Press, 1997).
C. Willink (ed.), *Euripides: Orestes* (Oxford: Clarendon Press, 1986).
C. Wilson, *The Outsider* (London: Gollancz, 1956).
P. Wilson, 'Tragedy in the Fourth Century', in P.E. Easterling (ed.), *The Cambridge Companion to Greek Tragedy* (Cambridge: Cambridge University Press, 1997).
——— (ed.), *Greek Theatre Rituals* (Oxford: Oxford University Press, 2007).
J.P. Winkler and F.I. Zeitlin (eds), *Nothing to Do with Dionysos? Athenian Drama in its Social Context* (Princeton: Princeton University Press, 1990).

Euripides: Orestes

R.P. Winnington-Ingram, 'Euripides: *poiêtês sophos*', *Arethusa* 2 (1969), pp. 127-42.

——— 'Tragica', *Bulletin of the Institute of Classical Studies* 16 (1969), pp. 44-54.

C. Wolff, '*Orestes*', in E. Segal (ed.), *Euripides* (Englewood Cliffs: Prentice-Hall, 1968), pp. 132-49; reprinted in E. Segal (ed.), *Oxford Readings in Greek Tragedy* (Oxford: Oxford University Press, 1983), pp. 340-56.

M.E. Wright, *Euripides' Escape-Tragedies: A Study of* Helen, Andromeda *and* Iphigenia among the Taurians (Oxford: Oxford University Press, 2005).

——— '*Orestes*, A Euripidean Sequel', *Classical Quarterly* 56 (2006), pp. 33-47.

——— 'Comedy and the Trojan War', *Classical Quarterly* 57 (2007), pp. 412-31.

——— '*Enter* a Phrygian (Euripides, *Orestes* 1369)', *Greek, Roman and Byzantine Studies* 48 (2008), pp. 5-13.

F.I. Zeitlin, 'The Closet of Masks: Role-playing and Myth-making in Euripides' *Orestes*', *Ramus* 9 (1980), pp. 51-77.

Glossary

aetiological: explanatory (from the Greek *aition*, an explanation). An 'aetiological' myth tends to be one which goes back in time to explain how some familiar feature of modern life came about.
agôn: a formal, courtroom-style debate between two central characters.
amoibaion: a sung duet.
anagnôrisis: recognition (often of long-lost relatives who are happily reunited).
antilabê: very quick dialogue, in which a single line of Greek verse is broken up between two or more speakers.
aulos: a woodwind instrument used widely in tragedy and other forms of Greek musical performance. The nearest modern equivalent is perhaps the oboe.
dêmos: the population (hence 'democracy', rule by the people as a whole).
deus ex machina: literally 'the god from the crane'. This phrase refers to the sudden appearance of a god, usually at the end of the play. The actor playing the god would be swung into view on the **mêchanê**. The phrase *deus ex machina* is Latin; the Greek equivalent is *theos apo tês mêchanês*.
deuteragonist: the second actor, with fewer lines than the **protagonist**.
Dionysia: festival of Dionysus, the god of theatre. Many of the tragedies and comedies we possess from antiquity were staged at the Greater (or 'City') Dionysia, a major spring festival which took place at Athens and attracted many foreign visitors to the city.
ekkyklêma: a small portable stage on wheels.
episode (Greek *epeisodion*; plural *epeisodia*): a scene, principally composed of dialogue, placed in between periods of singing and dancing.
Erinyes: the Greek name for the Furies (goddesses of vengeance).
fragment: a partial remnant of a lost work of literature. Fragments may take the form of quotations or citations in other ancient works,

or they may literally be scraps of papyrus or parchment discovered by archaeologists.

gnômê (plural ***gnômai***): a maxim or proverbial statement; common in tragedy; often cryptic in meaning.

hetaireia (plural ***hetaireiai***): a political club or faction, whose membership typically included discontented young aristocrats or oligarchic sympathizers. A member of such a group was called a ***hetairos*** or ***philos***.

hypothesis: an ancient plot-summary attached to the manuscript of a Greek play. The exact date and authorship of most *hypotheses* is unknown, and they are often unreliable, but they can contain useful information about the play's first production.

iambic trimeter: the **metre** used for standard scenes of 'normal' dialogue in tragedy. This metre was said to be the closest to everyday speech rhythm.

intertextuality: the (often self-conscious) relationship of one literary text to other texts.

kommos: a sung lament, often in the form of a duet.

kômôidia: the Greek name for the genre in which Aristophanes wrote: not the same as 'comedy' in a broader sense.

Lenaea: festival of Dionysus; smaller than the **Dionysia** and (probably) attended only by Athenians.

libation: an offering (in the context of religious ritual).

mêchanê: mechanical crane or harness, used for managing surprise entrances (especially entrances of a ***deus ex machina***).

metatheatricality: a highly self-conscious and self-referential technique whereby it is made clear that the play *is* a play and the characters are really actors. Often this technique is used as a way of commenting on the conventions of theatre or the nature of the theatrical illusion.

metre: the term used for the rhythmic pattern of poetry and song.

monody: a song performed by a solo actor (comparable to an operatic aria).

oligarch: one who believes in political rule by an elite minority.

orchêstra: in the Greek world, this word refers to the flat (circular or rectangular) area in the centre of the theatre, which was used for acting and dancing. The word 'stage' in English does not quite represent the right meaning, since there was no *raised* stage in the Greek theatre.

parabasis: a type of scene found in comedy (not tragedy), in which the leader of the chorus comes forward and addresses the audience, seemingly in the persona of the playwright.

parodos (plural ***parodoi***): this Greek word is used, confusingly, to mean (*a*) the song performed by the chorus on its first entry, and (*b*) the two ramps or passages which led onto the ***orchêstra*** from each

Glossary

side, allowing the characters to make their entrances and exits. It may be more convenient to refer to (*b*) by the alternative term *eisodoi*.

peripeteia: a 'reversal' or unexpected turnabout in events. A term used by Aristotle in his *Poetics*.

polis: a Greek city-state (whose members or citizens are called ***politai***).

prologue (Greek ***prologos***): everything that happens on stage before the first entry of the chorus.

protagonist: the 'star' actor, the one who had the most lines. (This word is often used, wrongly, to mean 'the main character'.)

shawm: a type of double-reeded woodwind instrument, with similarities to the modern oboe or bassoon.

skênê: the wooden stage-building at the rear of the acting area, which could be used to represent the palace (or other type of setting). The actors could use the *skênê* to make their entrances and exits and to change their costumes.

sophist: a controversial type of philosopher and rhetorician who sprung up at Athens in the last few decades of the fifth century BC. The most famous sophists were Gorgias and Protagoras; Socrates was often numbered among them, but he was anxious to distance himself from the group.

stasimon (plural ***stasima***): choral song in between scenes of dialogue.

stichomythia: rapid-fire dialogue in which each participant speaks one line at a time.

strophic: a term used to refer to verses of song which correspond to each other. Typically a choral ***stasimon*** will be made up of a pattern of **strophai** and **antistrophai** (verses which use the same **metre** and music as each other).

tragôidia: the Greek name for the genre to which *Orestes* belongs; not at all the same thing as other types of 'tragedy'.

tritagonist: the third actor.

tychê: chance, fortune or randomness.

Chronology

c. 480 Euripides' birth
462-   Radical democracy instituted at Athens
458   Aeschylus' *Oresteia*
c. 456 Death of Aeschylus
455   Euripides' first entry in the dramatic competition
438   Euripides' *Alcestis*
431   Outbreak of Peloponnesian War; Euripides' *Medea*
427   The sophist Gorgias arrives at Athens from Sicily
428   Euripides' *Hippolytus*
c. 415? Sophocles' *Electra;* Euripides' *Electra* (dates uncertain)
415   Athenians send expedition to Sicily; Euripides' *Trojan Women*
413   Invasion of Sicily is utterly defeated
412   Euripides' *Helen* and *Andromeda*
411   Oligarchic revolution at Athens;
         Aristophanes' *Women at the Thesmophoria*
410   Uncertain restoration of Athenian democracy
409   Sophocles' *Philoctetes*
408   Euripides' *Orestes*
406   Death of Euripides;
         Bacchae and *Iphigenia at Aulis* produced posthumously
405   Aristophanes' *Frogs*
404   End of Peloponnesian War: Athens defeated by Sparta.

Index

actors 13, 26, 30, 34, 38, 47, 48, 113, 120, 123-4
Aegisthus 22, 43, 57, 60-4, 112, 132-3
Aeschylus:
  life and works 15, 42, 43, 54
  Oresteia 15, 23, 25, 31, 48, 59-60, 64, 69, 70, 75, 79-82, 93, 97, 106, 122
  Persians 13, 79
aetiological myths 70-1
Agamemnon 22, 27, 58, 60-2, 79, 100, 112-13, 129
Agathon 24, 79
agôn-scenes 40-1, 54, 62-4, 97, 130-3
anachronism 24, 87-9
Anaxagoras 119, 134-6
Antiphon 102
Apollo 38, 48-50, 55, 61-2, 64-71, 99, 133
Archeptolemus 102
Archive of Performances of Greek and Roman Drama 14-15
Argos 24, 28, 34, 49, 59, 66, 69, 81, 88-9, 92, 103, 106-14, 126, 129, 135-6
Argive assembly 32-4, 40, 42, 59, 102-3, 106-9
Aristophanes
  life and works 10, 11, 39, 73, 85-6, 115-16, 125
  Clouds 118, 130, 135

Frogs 13, 73, 76, 82-3, 85, 94-5, 102-3, 130
Wasps 130
Aristotle 19, 31-3, 53, 76, 92
[Aristotle], *Athenian Constitution* 101-2, 148
Athens 24, 75-6, 88-9, 90-3, 98-103, 106-14, 130
Atreus 17, 21-2, 27, 41, 48, 60, 62, 136
audience 21, 25, 52, 59, 117-19, 121-2, 137
audience address 26, 33-5, 89, 120, 127

'Byzantine triad' 17

characterization 51-60, 70
chorus 13, 30, 36-7, 38-9, 41, 42, 44-5, 48, 60, 110-11, 126
Cleophon 102-3, 113
cleverness 15, 57, 115-24
closure 49-50, 69-71
Clytemnestra 17, 22, 27, 34, 39, 43, 53, 60-4, 79, 106, 111, 129, 132-3
comedy 9, 10, 30, 69, 92, 120-1, 139 (*see also* genre)
cosmology 26-7, 42, 122, 133-6
Cypria 23

dates of plays' first performance 9-11
demagogues 102-3, 113

173

Index

deus ex machina 30, 48-50, 64, 69-71, 114
Diomedes 108
Dionysia 9, 12, 90-1
Dionysus 9, 10, 12, 94
dramatic 'illusion' 25, 119-24

ekkyklêma 30, 45
Electra 25-8, 32, 33-6, 41, 42, 44-5, 53-4, 69, 82, 100, 104-6, 107-13, 120-2, 125-6, 127-8, 134-6
Empedocles 135-6
epic cycle 23, 81 (*see also* Cypria; Nostoi)
Erinyes see Furies
ethics 50-1, 54-7, 60-4, 105-6, 131-3
Euripides:
 life and works 10-11, 64-6, 72-7, 87, 144
 Alcestis 11, 25
 Andromache 49, 84, 98
 Andromeda 84, 118, 123
 Antiope 32
 Bacchae 11, 16, 19, 49, 73, 76-7, 97
 Children of Heracles 93, 114
 Electra 23, 49, 53, 54, 86, 110
 Hecuba 98
 Helen 10, 19, 24, 25, 32, 39, 44, 49, 57-8, 77, 81-3, 84, 98-9, 115, 118, 123, 128-9
 Heracles 11, 56
 Hippolytus 10, 25, 49, 110
 Hypsipyle 84
 Ion 19, 20, 24, 49, 64, 77
 Iphigenia at Aulis 11, 23, 76-7, 81, 98
 Iphigenia among the Taurians 15, 20, 23, 24, 32, 49, 53, 64, 77, 81, 98, 118
 Medea 10, 11, 19, 25, 81
 Phoenician Women 49, 77
 Rhesus 11, 49, 145

Suppliant Women 49, 93, 114
Trojan Women 11, 98-9

'false preparation' 34, 38, 44-5
female characters in Euripides 54
friendship 40, 42, 57, 67, 103-6
Furies (*Erinyes*) 34, 38, 55, 67-8, 129

genre 18-20, 73-7, 78, 118-24, 127 (*see also* comedy; tragedy)
gnômai (maxims) 26, 126
gods 52, 58, 62, 64-8, 99, 114, 132-3, 136 (*see also* Apollo, Zeus etc.)
Gorgias 99, 116, 128

Hegelochus 38
Helen 24, 34, 43-5, 46, 49, 57-8, 63, 69-71, 81-3, 99, 111-12, 128-9
Hermione 24, 34, 43-5, 48-9, 59-60, 63, 69, 81, 100-1, 111-12
Heraclitus 122, 135-6
heroism 99-101
Hesiod 23
hetaireiai (political clubs) 103-6
Homer 23, 60, 63, 81, 135

ideology 93-6, 114
incongruity 24, 28, 33, 42, 43, 48, 81
illness and insanity 18, 33-6, 54-6
intelligence 56-7, 59, 66-8, 131-2
intertextuality 36, 48, 79-83, 122-4
Iphigenia 22, 79
irony 24, 69-71, 115, 121, 125, 126

'late' style 13-14, 21, 72-89, 101

mêchanê (mechanical crane) 14, 46, 49
'*mêchanêma*-plots' 32
Menander 16

174

Index

Menelaus 24, 34, 39, 41, 47-9, 54, 58-9, 61-4, 65, 69, 81-2, 100-11, 111-13, 125
messengers 42, 46, 107, 113, 125
'metamythology' 127
metatheatricality 25-8, 119-24, 124-6, 127, 150
'modern-dress' tragedy 87-9 (*see also* anachronism)
music 24, 36-7, 38-9, 45-7, 142, 146 (*see also* 'New Music')
Myrtilus 22, 62
myth 15, 21-4, 44, 53, 58, 79, 114, 127-8

Neoptolemus 16
'New Music' 37, 46-7, 83-7, 125
Nietzsche, F. 19, 21, 73-7, 118
Nostoi 23
novelty 21-4, 31, 83-9, 115, 124-6

Oeax 112
Oenomaus 22, 62
oligarchy 101-3, 104-6
Orestes 21, 22, 26, 28, 32-4, 38, 39, 42, 47-9, 53, 54-8, 59, 60-4, 65, 69, 102-3, 103-6, 107-9, 111-13, 129, 130-3

parody 139
Peloponnesian War 75-6, 98-101, 114
Pelops 22, 62
performance 15, 16, 29-31, 33-50
peripeteia (reversal) 13, 32-3
Pherecrates 86
philosophy 82, 116-17, 117-19, 126-37
Phrygian slave 20, 45-7, 60, 84-5, 100-1, 122-3, 126
Phrynichus 109
Pindar 23, 28
Plato 86, 95, 113
plot-structure 20, 24, 25, 31-50, 78

politics 12, 75, 88-9, 90-114
prologue 25-8, 33-6, 140
Pylades 40, 43, 44, 48-9, 57, 69, 103-6, 113, 124, 129

realism 12, 24, 28, 53, 120
reality *versus* illusion 24, 53, 82-3, 98, 120-1, 124, 126-30
reception 14-18, 35-6, 41, 47, 49-50, 65-6, 74-5, 87-9, 98, 115-16
recognition 13
revenge 60-4 (*see also* ethics)
rhetoric 116-17, 130-3
ritual 12, 68, 71, 94, 127-8

satyr-drama 9
scholarship, ancient 10, 16, 17, 34, 39, 45, 52, 60, 70, 72-3, 87, 142
sequels 23, 57-8, 79-83, 101, 128-9
skênê (stage-building) 13, 29-31, 33, 44-5, 47
Socrates 115-16, 118
solo singing 13, 36, 45-7
sophists 116-17, 128, 130-3
Sophocles:
  life and works 11, 13, 23, 25, 43, 54
  Antigone 15, 31, 97
  Electra 23, 53, 55-7, 80-1, 125
  Oedipus the King 15, 19, 31
staging 33-50 (*see also* performance)
Stesichorus 23, 28, 80, 125
Strattis 15, 115-16
sunesis 56-7

Talthybius 103, 108
Tantalus 22, 26, 62, 134-5
textual transmission 17
textual problems 35, 39, 41, 44, 45, 49, 108, 113, 149, 150-1
Theatre of Dionysus 9, 29-31

175

Index

Theramenes 103, 108
Thucydides 98-9, 101-2, 104-6, 107, 111, 113, 114, 130
Thyestes 22, 41, 61, 136
Timotheus 86-7, 125
'tone' 24, 37, 46-7, 60, 119-24
tragedy 11-14, 18-20, 74-7, 87, 90, 96, 118-24
trilogies 139
Trojan War 34, 57, 60-2, 70-1, 81-2, 98-101, 112

tychê (fortune) 33, 67-8
Tyndareus 23, 39, 54, 59, 108-9, 131-3

Vergil 16

[Xenophon], *Athenian Constitution* ('The Old Oligarch') 113, 114

Zeus 22, 70, 85, 99

www.ingramcontent.com/pod-product-compliance
Lightning Source LLC
Chambersburg PA
CBHW051101230426
43667CB00013B/2394